EUROPEAN STUDIES

SECOND EDITION

Maria Williams and Dave Pearce

Hodder & Stoughton

A MEMBER OF THE HODDER HEADLINE GROUP

Orders: please contact Bookpoint Ltd, 39 Milton Park, Abingdon, Oxon OX14 4TD. Telephone: (44) 01235 400414, Fax: (44) 01235 400454. Lines are open from 9.00–6.00, Monday to Saturday, with a 24 hour message answering service. Email address: orders@bookpoint.co.uk

A catalogue record for this title is available from The British Library

ISBN 0 340 701463

First published 1998
Impression number   10 9 8 7 6 5 4 3 2 1
Year   2004 2003 2002 2001 1999 1998

Cover montage created by Stefan Brazzo

Typeset by Fakenham Photosetting Limited, Fakenham, Norfolk NR21 8NL
Printed in Great Britain for Hodder & Stoughton Educational, a division of Hodder Headline Plc, 338 Euston Road, London NW1 3BH by Scotprint, Musselburgh, Scotland.

Contents

Country Profiles

Introduction

It would be difficult to imagine life today in the UK without membership of the European Union. For better or worse, in spite of the media fixation with the spectre of a Brussels superpower, the UK is now inextricably linked to its European partners in terms of trade, politics and future prosperity. Early indications are that the Labour government elected in 1997 will seek to play a more significant role in Europe than that played by the previous Conservative government.

By 1998, the UK will have had full membership of the European Union for 25 years. It has been a turbulent relationship in some ways, but, approaching the Millennium the relationship appears to be maturing. The 50th anniversary of the founding of the European Union is not too far away in 2007. The latter half of the century has seen an incredible change in the political and economic scene in Europe. From the ruins of the Second World War, the six founder members nurtured and gave birth to the fledgling European Economic Community in 1957. The following calendar gives brief details of the creation of the EEC and its gradual enlargement.

CALENDAR FOR THE CREATION OF THE EUROPEAN UNION

1946 Discussion of United States of Europe by Winston Churchill. Churchill urged other European states to band together to prevent future disputes.

1947 Marshall Plan gives financial aid to Europe from USA. The aid was pledged to help rebuild Europe, providing the Europeans could find some mechanism for working together.

1951 European Coal and Steel Community formed by Germany and France. This first cooperative act linked their respective industries and formed a 'common market' for these goods.

1957 Original six sign the Treaty of Rome to create the EEC – France, Germany, Belgium, The Netherlands, Luxembourg and Italy.

1959 Britain creates EFTA (European Free Trade Association) as a competitive organisation to the EEC and to protect Commonwealth interests.

1961 First British application to join the EEC.

1963	France vetoes the UK's application.
1967	Second application from the UK, again refused by France.
1973	UK joins the EEC along with Ireland and Denmark.
1981	Greece joins.
1986	Spain and Portugal join.
	The Single European Act launches the Single European Market (effective 1 January 1993) and gives European integration a boost in trade terms.
1992	The Maastricht Treaty launched the European Union, binding the member states more closely together.
1995	Sweden, Austria and Finland join.

The development of the EEC to the EU is covered in detail in Chapter 3.

From its post-war origins, the Community was created to avoid future disputes and wars, to enhance European prosperity and to provide a world power able to take on the formidable might of the superpowers (the USSR, USA and, in trade terms, Japan). The Community's development has progressed in fits and starts. There have been periods when developments have been achieved slowly and with difficulty, for example the 1970s and other times, the late 1980s when progress has been achieved much more quickly. Today, the Maastricht Treaty has presented an ambitious programme which amply demonstrates the member states' ambitions.

- Monetary union by 1999
- New common policies
- European citizenship
- A common foreign and security policy and internal security
- Major initiatives to tackle unemployment and maintain competitiveness
- Increased powers for the European parliament

The above list is ambitious, but forms the basis of the programme designed to carry the EU into the twenty-first century. The member states are serious in their desire to achieve the Maastricht programme and determined to do so. Their record of achievement over the past 40 years is enviable and leaves little doubt that progress will be made to ensure that Maastricht's principles are enacted.

A Guide to the Country Profiles

Each country section opens with a map. This is followed by the first table, which sets out some basic information about the country: its size (land area) and capital city, the currency used, language(s) spoken and religion(s) practised, and the head of state and current prime minister.

The *Population Profile* gives the size of the country's total population, the size of its active or working population, how this population relates to the size of the country and how it breaks down in terms of age.

The *Economic Profile* gives basic information about the country's economic activity: its gross national product, largest companies, imports and exports, and the name of its central bank.

KEY TO THE ECONOMIC PROFILE TABLES

CIF **Cost, Insurance and Freight**
This means that the seller/exporter will pay for freight and insurance charges to a named port; all charges thereafter will be borne by the purchaser/importer

FOB **Free On Board**
This means that the seller/exporter is responsible for the costs of delivering goods to the ship, but all costs thereafter are borne by the purchaser/importer.

GNP **Gross National Product**
The amount of goods and services a country produces, expressed in money terms and usually measured per year.

The *Political Profile* briefly describes the system of central and local government and outlines the results of the most recent elections.

Other tables then give information on *The Transport Infrastructure*: the size of road and rail networks, the names of national airlines, *Communications*: details of the major broadcast and printed news media, and *International Relations*: a list of the international organisations to which each country belongs.

INTERNATIONAL ORGANISATIONS: ABBREVIATIONS USED IN THE COUNTRY PROFILES

EEA **European Economic Area**
An association between the EU and EFTA countries, focusing on free trade and certain aspects of the Single European Act.

NATO **North Atlantic Treaty Organisation**
As association, created in 1949, of Western countries dedicated to maintaining a single mutual defence system.

OECD	**Organisation for Economic Cooperation and Development**
	An organisation formed to encourage growth and help stabilise exchange rates.
Schengen Accord	An agreement among certain European states to lift border controls.
UN	**United Nations**
	An association of states formed in 1945 to foster international peace and security.
WEU	**Western European Union**
	An association of states formed in 1948, dedicated to collaboration on economic, social and cultural affairs and on joint self-defence.

For more information on the role of European nations, and of the EU as a whole, in these international bodies, see Chapter 9.

Austria

Land Area	83,855 sq. km.
Capital	Vienna
Currency	Schilling
Languages	German
Religion	75% Roman Catholic
Head of State (President)	Thomas Klestil
Federal Chancellor	Franz Vranitzky

POPULATION PROFILE

Population (1995)	8 million

Labour Force (1994)

Labour Force (000s)	3,877	as a percentage of population	48.3

Civilians in Employment by Sector

	%		%
Agriculture, forestry, fishing	7.0	Wholesale, retail, restaurants, hotels	19.5
Mining, quarrying	0.3	Transport, storage, communications	6.6
Manufacturing	22.5	Finance, insurance, real estate, business services	9.2
Electricity, gas, water	0.9	Community, social, personal services	23.9
Construction	9.8	Not defined	–

Unemployment Rate (1996)

4.2%

Population by age and sex (1995)

Age Group	Total 000s	Total %	Male 000s	Male %	Female 000s	Female %
0–4	469	5.8	241	3.0	229	2.8
5–9	464	5.8	238	3.0	226	2.8
10–14	479	6.0	245	3.0	234	2.9
15–24	1,019	12.7	518	6.4	500	6.2
25–34	1,421	17.7	730	9.1	691	8.6
35–44	1,149	14.3	587	7.3	562	7.0
45–54	1,019	12.7	511	6.4	508	6.3
55–64	808	10.0	391	4.9	418	5.2
65+	1,218	15.1	441	5.5	777	9.7
Total	**8,047**	**100.0**	**3,902**	**48.5**	**4,144**	**51.5**

Population per sq. km.

93.0

ECONOMIC PROFILE

GNP per capita, Schillings (1995)	290.0			

5 biggest companies (1994)

Rank	Company	Sector	Turnover Sch. million	No. of Employees
1	ÖMV	Chemicals	67,958	29,141
2	Öst. Post/ Telegraphenverw	Transport	61,098	56,983
3	VA Stahl AG	Metal industry	39,105	15,410
4	BML Vermögens- verwaltungs	Retail	35,072	15,444
5	Siemens Österreich	Electrical	33,217	18,234

Value of exports FOB, US$ bn (1994)

44.9

Value of imports CIF, US$ bn (1994)

55.1

Central bank

National Bank of Austria

POLITICAL PROFILE

Constitution/ electoral system	Federal democratic republic. Bicameral parliament – the *Nationalrat* with 183 members elected every 4 years by proportional representation and the *Bundesrat* with 63 members elected for various terms by the state legislature.
Local government	9 *Länder* (states) each with own state legislature and government
Last election	December 1995
Results	Social Democrats 71 People's Party (Conservative) 52 Freedom Party 42 Greens 9 Liberal Forum 10

INTERNATIONAL RELATIONS

Austria is a member of:	UN, EU, Council of Europe, OECD, the Partnership for Peace, NATO and the Schengen Accord.

TRANSPORT INFRASTRUCTURE

Rail	5,813 km. of railways in 1994 (nationalised). Also 19 private railways.
Road	10,207 km. of federal roads. 4,722,520 vehicles registered in 1994.
Air	Austrian Airlines. 6 international airports.

COMMUNICATIONS

Newspapers	17 daily newspapers with a circulation of 3.1 million in 1992.
TV/Radio	Austrian Broadcasting Corporation is state-controlled. Private TV broadcasting is not permitted. 4 national and 9 regional radio programmes. 2 TV programmes transmitted.

$\mathcal{B}elgium$

Land Area	30,519 sq. km.
Capital	Brussels
Currency	Belgian Franc (BFr) of 100 centimes
Languages	Flemish, French and German
Religion	75% Roman Catholic
Head of State	King Albert II
Prime Minister	Jean-Luc Dehaene

POPULATION PROFILE

Population (1995)	10.1 million

Labour Force (1995)

Labour force (000s)	4,184	as a percentage of population	41.3

Civilians in Employment by Sector	%		%
Agriculture, forestry	3.0	Wholesale, retail, restaurants, hotels	18.1
Mining, quarrying	0.3	Transport, storage, communications	7.6
Manufacturing	23.3	Finance, insurance, business services	9.4
Electricity, gas, water	0.9	Community, social, personal services	30.4
Construction	7.0		

Unemployment Rate (1996)

9.9%

Population by age and sex (1995)

Age Group	Total 000s	%	Male 000s	%	Female 000s	%
0–4	615	6.1	315	3.1	300	3.0
5–9	603	6.0	309	3.1	294	2.9
10–14	609	6.0	312	3.1	297	2.9
15–24	1,299	12.8	661	6.5	638	6.3
25–34	1,572	15.5	801	7.9	771	7.6
35–44	1,507	14.9	765	7.6	742	7.3
45–54	1,218	12.0	614	6.0	604	6.0
55–64	1,112	11.0	539	5.3	573	5.7
65+	1,596	15.7	639	6.3	967	9.4
Total	**10,131**	**100.0**	**4,955**	**48.9**	**5,176**	**51.1**

Population per sq. km.

331.8

ECONOMIC PROFILE

GNP per capita, BFr (1995)	928,000

5 biggest companies (1994)

Rank	Company	Sector	Turnover BFr million	No. of Employees
1	Petrofina	Petroleum	558,391	14,013
2	Delhaize de Lion	Retail	380,620	83,805
3	Tractebel	Power/general	297,777	36,309
4	Solvay	Chemicals	262,227	41,314
5	GB Inno–BM Group	Retail	232,460	45,604

Value of exports FOB, US$ bn (1995)	169.2
Value of imports CIF, US$ bn (1995)	154.8
Central bank	National Bank

POLITICAL PROFILE

Constitution/ electoral system	Constitutional monarchy. Chamber of Representatives (lower house) has 150 members elected every 4 years. Senate (upper house) has 71 members.
Local government	Belgium is divided into 10 provinces and 589 communes. Communal councils are elected every 6 years. The President of the commune is the 'Burgomaster' and is assisted by 'aldermen'.
Last election	May 1995
Results	Flemish Christian Social Party (CVP) 29 Flemish Liberal and Democratic Party (VLD) 21 Francophone Socialist (PS) 21 Flemish Socialist (SP) 20 Francophone Liberal Reform Party – Democratic Front of Francophones (PRL–FDF) 18 Francophone Christian Social Party 12 Viaams Blok (VB) 11 Francophone Ecology Party (ECOLO) 6 Volksunie (VU) 5 Flemish Ecology Party (AGALEV) 5 National Front 2

INTERNATIONAL RELATIONS

Belgium is a member of:	UN, EU, Council of Europe, NATO, OECD & WEU and the Schengen Accord.

TRANSPORT INFRASTRUCTURE

Rail	Société Nationale des Chemins de Fer Belges (SNCB) 1994, 3,396 km.
Road	1,665 km. motorways in 1995. 5,136,342 vehicles registered in 1995.
Air	SABENA is the national airline. 2 international airports.

COMMUNICATIONS	
Newspapers	33 daily newspapers (18 French, 14 Dutch and 1 German) in 1993. Circulation of 2,057,169 in 1992.
TV/Radio	Public services BRTN, RTBF and BRF broadcast in Dutch, French and German respectively (radio and TV). There are 3 commercial networks: VTM, RTL–TVI and Canal Plus.

Denmark

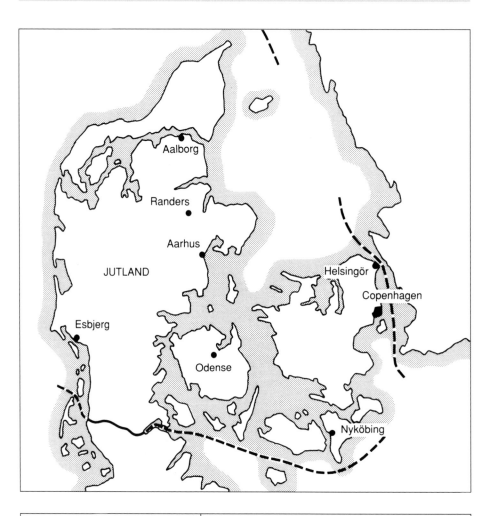

Land Area	43,080 sq. km.
Capital	Copenhagen
Currency	Danish Kroner (DKr) of 100 øre
Languages	Danish
Religion	97% Evangelical Lutheran
Head of State	Queen Margrethe II
Prime Minister	Poul Rasmussen

POPULATION PROFILE

Population (1995)	5.2 million

Labour Force (1994)

Labour force (000s)	2,893	as a percentage of population	55.8

Civilians in Employment by Sector	%		%
Agriculture, forestry, fishing	5.1	Wholesale, retail, restaurants, hotels	15.8
Mining, quarrying	0.1	Transport, storage, communications	7.2
Manufacturing	19.4		
Electricity, gas, water	0.6	Finance, insurance, real estate, business services	10.1
Construction	6.8	Community, social, personal services	34.6
		Not defined	0.3

Unemployment Rate (1996)

6.3%

Population by age and sex (1995)

Age Group	Total 000s	%	Male 000s	%	Female 000s	%
0–4	335	6.4	172	3.3	163	3.1
5–9	292	5.6	150	2.9	142	2.7
10–14	274	5.3	140	2.7	134	2.6
15–24	702	13.5	358	6.9	344	6.6
25–34	807	15.5	414	7.9	393	7.5
35–44	742	14.2	377	7.2	364	7.0
45–54	753	14.4	381	7.3	371	7.1
55–64	513	9.8	251	4.8	261	5.0
65+	799	15.3	330	6.3	469	9.0
Total	**5,216**	**100.0**	**2,573**	**49.3**	**2,642**	**50.7**

Population per sq. km.

121.0

ECONOMIC PROFILE

GNP per capita, DKr (1995)	945.2

5 biggest companies (1994)

Rank	Company	Sector	Turnover DKr million	No. of Employees
1	Borealis	Agency/commis	15,615	–
2	FLS Industries	Holding co.s	14,477	–
3	Danisco	Drink/ confectionery	12,844	–
4	Det Østasiatiske Kompagni	Wholesaler	12,450	–
5	MD Foods Amba	Dairy products	12,182	6,222

Value of exports FOB, US$ bn (1995)	49.1
Value of imports CIF, US$ bn (1995)	43.7
Central bank	National Bank

POLITICAL PROFILE

Constitution/ electoral system	Constitutional monarchy. Single chamber parliament (*Folketing*) has 179 members elected under a system of proportional representation every 4 years.
Local government	275 municipalities (*kommuner*), each with a district council of between 7 and 31 members and an elected mayor. 14 counties each with county council and elected mayor. Local elections every 4 years. The Faroe Islands and Greenland are governed under a system of home rule.
Last election	September 1994
Results (seats in *Folketing*)	Social Democratic Party (SD) 62

Liberal Party	42
Conservative Party	27
Socialist Party	13
Progress Party	11
Social Liberal Party (SL)	8
Red–Green Alliance	6
Centre Democrats (CD)	5

INTERNATIONAL RELATIONS

Denmark is a member of:	UN, NATO, OECD, EU, Council of Europe and the Nordic Council.

TRANSPORT INFRASTRUCTURE

Rail	2,349 km. of state railways in 1994.
Road	786 km. of motorways in 1995. 1,610,955 vehicles registered in 1995.
Air	SAS state airline. 1 international airport at Copenhagen.

COMMUNICATIONS

Newspapers	37 daily newspapers with a combined circulation of 1.62 million in 1994.
TV/Radio	Television is broadcast by Danmarks Radio and TV2.

Finland

Land Area	388,142 sq. km.
Capital	Helsinki
Currency	Finnish Markka (FMk)
Languages	Finnish and Swedish
Religion	86% Lutheran
Head of State (President)	Martti Ahtisaari
Prime Minister	Paavo Lipponen

POPULATION PROFILE

Population (1995)	5.1 million

Labour Force (1994)

Labour force (000s)	2,502	as a percentage of population	49.2

Civilians in Employment by Sector	%		%
Agriculture, forestry, fishing	8.2	Transport, storage, communications	8.0
Mining, quarrying	0.2	Finance, insurance, real estate, business services	10.0
Manufacturing	19.7		
Electricity, gas, water	1.1	Community, social, personal services	32.1
Construction	5.6	Not defined	0.4
Wholesale retail, restaurants, hotels	14.7		

Unemployment Rate (1996)

16.1%

Population by age and sex (1995)

Age Group	Total 000s	%	Male 000s	%	Female 000s	%
0–4	325	6.3	165	3.2	159	3.1
5–9	317	6.2	162	3.2	155	3.0
10–14	330	6.5	169	3.3	161	3.2
15–24	632	12.4	323	6.3	309	6.0
25–34	727	14.2	371	7.3	356	7.0
35–44	789	15.4	402	7.8	387	7.6
45–54	756	14.8	383	7.5	373	7.3
55–64	509	9.9	246	4.8	263	5.1
65+	732	14.3	271	5.3	461	9.0
Total	**5,117**	**100.0**	**2,492**	**48,7**	**2,625**	**51.3**

Population per sq. km.	17.0

ECONOMIC PROFILE

GNP per capita, FMk billion (1994)	485.6

5 biggest companies (1995)

Rank	Company	Sector	Turnover FMk million	No. of Employees
1	Neste	Chemicals & plastics	43,335	8,840
2	Nokia	Electronics & electrical equip.	36,810	31,948
3	Repola	General	33,197	28,138
4	Kesko	Retail	26,439	5,833
5	Kymmene	Forest & paper products	21,541	17,594

Value of exports FOB, US$ bn (1995)	40.0
Value of imports CIF, US$ bn (1995)	28.9
Central bank	Bank of Finland

POLITICAL PROFILE

Constitution/ electoral system	Independent republic. Uni-cameral parliament (*Eduskunta*). 200 members elected by system of proportional representation for 4 years. President elected for 6-year term.
Local government	12 provinces each administered by a governor appointed by the President.
Last election	1995
Results	Finnish Social Democratic Party 63 Centre Party 44 National Coalition Party 39 Left-Wing Alliance 22 Swedish People's Party 12 The Greens 9 Finnish Christian Union 7 Progressive Liberal Finns 2 Finnish Rural Party 1

INTERNATIONAL RELATIONS

Finland is a member of:	UN, EU, Nordic Council, OECD, Council of Europe and the NATO Partnership for Peace.

TRANSPORT INFRASTRUCTURE

Rail	5,859 km. of railways in 1994.
Road	79,166 km. of public roads in 1995. 1,872,588 cars registered in 1994.
Air	Finnair is the national airline. 1 international airport at Helsinki.

COMMUNICATIONS

Newspapers	56 newspapers published more than 3 times per week (8 in Swedish language).
TV/Radio	4 TV programmes (1 of which is commercial). 59 local radio stations and 186 private cable networks.

France

Land Area	544,000 sq. km.
Capital	Paris
Currency	French Franc (FFr) of 100 centimes
Languages	French
Religion	90% Roman Catholic
Head of State	President Jaques Chirac
Prime Minister	Lionel Jospin

POPULATION PROFILE

Population (1996)	58.2 million

Labour Force (1994)

Labour force (000s)	25,385	as a percentage of population	43.8

Civilians in Employment by Sector

	%		%
Agriculture, forestry, fishing	4.7	Wholesale, retail, restaurants, hotels	16.8
Mining, quarrying	0.3	Transport, storage, communications	6.3
Manufacturing	18.8		
Electricity, gas, water	0.9	Finance, insurance, real estate, business services	10.6
Construction	6.5	Community, social, personal services	35.0
		Not defined	0.1

Unemploy-ment Rate (1996)	11.5%

Population by age and sex (1995)

Age Group	Total 000s	%	Male 000s	%	Female 000s	%
0–4	3,594	6.2	1,838	3.2	1,756	3.0
5–9	3,833	6.6	1,961	3.4	1,872	3.2
10–14	3,885	6.7	1,988	3.4	1,897	3.3
15–24	8,021	13.8	4,076	7.0	3,945	6.8
25–34	8,662	14.9	4,340	7.4	4,323	7.4
35–44	8,559	14.7	4,257	7.3	4,302	7.4
45–54	7,192	12.3	3,616	6.2	3,576	6.1
55–64	5,654	9.8	2,736	4.7	2,918	5.0
65+	8,863	15.2	3,559	6.1	5,304	9.1
Total	**58,265**	**100.0**	**28,370**	**48.7**	**29,895**	**51.3**

Population per sq. km.	107.1

ECONOMIC PROFILE

GNP per capita, FFr billion (1994)

7,325

5 biggest companies (1995)

Rank	Company	Sector	Turnover FFr. million	No. of Employees
1	Elf Aquitaine	Petroleum	208,290	85,500
2	Electricité de France	Power	188,553	118,707
3	Renault	Automotive	184,065	139,950
4	P.S.A. Citroën Peugeot	Automotive	164,248	139,900
5	Générale des Eaux	Water, energy, media	160,589	221,157

Value of exports FOB, US$ bn (1995)

286.7

Value of imports CIF, US$ bn (1995)

266.7

Central bank

Banque de France

POLITICAL PROFILE

Constitution/ electoral system	Republic. System of government based on the Constitution of the Fifth Republic. President is elected every 7 years. National Assembly (lower house) has 577 deputies elected every 5 years. Senate (upper house) has 321 senators indirectly elected by electoral colleges in *départements*.
Local government	22 regions each with directly elected regional council. Regions made up of 96 *départements* and 36,551 communes. Each commune is run by an elected municipal council which elects its own mayor. The Mayor represents both the commune and central government.
Last election	June 1997
Results	Socialists 241 Gaullists (RPR) 134 Union for French Democracy (UDF) 108 Communist Party (PCF) 38 Other left 21 Other right 14 Radical Socialist (MRG) 12 Ecologists 8 National Front 1

INTERNATIONAL RELATIONS

France is a member of:	UN, Council of Europe, NATO, WEU and EU.

TRANSPORT INFRASTRUCTURE

Rail	Société Nationale des Chemins de Fer Français (SNCF) has 32,275 km.
Road	354,000 km of departmental roads and 28,000 national road networks in 1992. 24 million private cars in 1992.
Air	Air France and Air Inter. 9 international airports.

COMMUNICATIONS	
Newspapers	77 daily newspapers. Total national daily circulation in 1993 came to 1.6 million.
TV/Radio	4 major radio stations. 2 state-owned channels and 5 commercial channels.

Germany

Land Area	357,000 sq. km.
Capital	Berlin
Currency	Deutschmark (DM) of 100 pfennig
Languages	German
Religion	50% Protestant 50% Roman Catholic
Head of State (President)	Roman Herzog
Federal Chancellor	Helmut Kohl

POPULATION PROFILE

Population (1996)

81.5 million

Labour Force (1994)

Labour force (000s)	39,628	as a percentage of population	48.7

Civilians in Employment by Sector

	%		%
Agriculture, forestry, fishing	3.3	Wholesale, retail, restaurants, hotels	14.9
Mining, quarrying	0.7	Transport, storage, communications	6.0
Manufacturing	26.7	Finance, insurance, real estate, business services	8.8
Electricity, gas, water	1.0		
Construction	8.6	Community, social, personal services	29.9
		Not defined	0.1

Unemploy-ment Rate (1996)

8.9%

Population by age and sex (1995)

Age Group	Total 000s	%	Male 000s	%	Female 000s	%
0–4	4,191	5.1	2,151	2.6	2,040	2.5
5–9	4,609	5.7	2,365	2.9	2,244	2.8
10–14	4,495	5.5	2,305	2.8	2,189	2.7
15–24	9,298	11.4	4,778	5.9	4,520	5.5
25–34	14,070	17.3	7,290	8.9	6,780	8.3
35–44	11,931	14.6	6,101	7.5	5,830	7.1
45–54	10,290	12.6	5,218	6.4	5,072	6.2
55–64	10,114	12.4	4,988	6.1	5,126	6.3
65+	12,542	15.4	4,450	5.5	8,092	9.9
Total	81,539	100.0	39,645	48.6	41,894	51.4

Population per sq. km.

228

ECONOMIC PROFILE

| **GNP per capita, DM billion (1994)** | 2,945 |

| **5 biggest companies (1995)** |

Rank	Company	Sector	Turnover DM million	No. of Employees
1	Daimler-Benz	Automotive	103,549	311,000
2	Siemens	Electrical equipment	88,763	376,100
3	Volkswagen	Automotive	88,119	242,000
4	Deutsche Telekom	Telecommunications	69,455	220,000
5	Metro-Gruppe	Retail, general	66,743	178,600

| **Value of exports FOB, US$ bn (1995)** | 511.0 |

| **Value of imports CIF, US$ bn (1995)** | 447.4 |

| **Central bank** | Deutsche Bundesbank |

POLITICAL PROFILE

Constitution/ electoral system	Federal republic *Bundestag* (federal assembly, lower house) has 672 members elected every 4 years *Bundesrat* (federal council, upper house) has 79 members appointed by *Länder* governments.
Local government	Germany comprises 16 *Länder* (states) divided into a total of 29 administrative districts. Each state has a constitution which complies with the Federal Basic Law. There are 426 counties (*Landkreise*), 117 county boroughs (*Kriesfreien Städte*) and 16,127 communities (*Gemeinden*).
Last election	October 1994
Results	Christian Democratic Union/Christian Social Union (CDU/CSU) 294 Social Democratic Party (SPD) 252 Greens 49 Free Democratic Party 47 Party for Democratic Socialists (PDS, formerly Communists) 30

INTERNATIONAL RELATIONS

Germany is a member of:	UN, OECD, EU, WEU, NATO, Council of Europe and Schengen Accord.

TRANSPORT INFRASTRUCTURE

Rail	40,355 km. in 1994.
Road	227,200 km. of classified roads in 1994. 46.8 million motor vehicles in 1995.
Air	Lufthansa is the national carrier. 12 international airports.

COMMUNICATIONS

Newspapers	392 newspapers in 1992 with a joint circulation of 31.3 million.
TV/Radio	12 regional radio and TV networks. 4 commercial TV networks. 2 public TV channels. 1 cable TV network.

Greece

Land Area	131,990 sq. km.
Capital	Athens
Currency	Drachma (Dra)
Languages	Greek
Religion	98% Christian Eastern Orthodox
Head of State (President)	Costis Stefanopoulos
Prime Minister	Costas Simitis

POPULATION PROFILE

Population (1995)	10.4 million

Labour Force (1995)

Labour force (000s)	4,248	as a percentage of population 40.7

Civilians in Employment by Sector

	%		%
Agriculture, forestry, fishing	20.5	Wholesale, retail, restaurants, hotels	22.2
Mining, quarrying	0.4	Transport, storage, communications	6.5
Manufacturing	15.1		
Electricity, gas, water	1.1	Finance, insurance, real estate, business services	6.3
Construction	6.6	Community, social, personal services	21.4

Unemployment Rate (1996)

9.1%

Population by age and sex (1995)

Age Group	Total 000s	%	Male 000s	%	Female 000s	%
0–4	519	5.0	268	2.6	251	2.4
5–9	572	5.5	294	2.8	278	2.7
10–14	694	6.6	357	3.4	337	3.2
15–24	1,557	14.9	799	7.7	758	7.3
25–34	1,549	14.8	778	7.4	772	7.4
35–44	1,418	13.6	709	6.8	708	6.8
45–54	1,249	12.0	620	5.9	629	6.0
55–64	1,280	12.3	619	5.9	661	6.3
65+	1,605	15.4	713	6.8	893	8.6
Total	**10,443**	**100.0**	**5,156**	**49.4**	**5,287**	**50.6**

Population per sq. km.

79.1

ECONOMIC PROFILE

GNP per capita, Dra billion (1994)	27,084

5 most profitable companies (1994)

Rank	Company	Sector	Net income Dra (000s)
1	Duty Free Shops S.A.	Misc. commodities	12,395,748
2	Procter & Gamble Hellas	Pharm/chemicals	5,605,822
3	Eko Fuels & Lubricants	Petroleum products	5,501,769
4	Shell Company (Hellas)	Petroleum products	5,187,823
5	Unisys Information Systems	Information systems	4,243,339

Value of exports FOB, US$ bn (1994)	9.5
Value of imports CIF, US$ bn (1994)	22.1
Central bank	Bank of Greece

POLITICAL PROFILE

Constitution/ electoral system	Republic. Parliamentary democracy led by ceremonial president. Simple chamber parliament (*Vouli*) of 300 members, elected every 4 years.
Local government	The Republic is divided into 359 towns, 52 prefectures, 13 regions and 5,600 wards. The Mayor is the recognised public figure in local government.
Last election	September 1996
Results	Socialists (PASOK) 162 New Democracy (ND) 110 Others 28

INTERNATIONAL RELATIONS

Greece is a member of:	UN, EU, WEU, Council of Europe and NATO and the Schengen Accord.

TRANSPORT INFRASTRUCTURE

Rail	Hellenic Railway (state network) had 2,484 km. in 1992.
Road	38,606 km. of roads in 1992. Number of vehicles: 2,807,447 in 1993.
Air	Olympic Airways. 2 international airports.

COMMUNICATIONS

Newspapers	117 daily newspapers in 1998.
TV/Radio	ERT is the government broadcasting station. 4 national and regional programmes. 2 TV programmes.

Ireland

Land Area	68,900 sq. km.
Capital	Dublin
Currency	Irish Pound (IR.£) or Punt in Eire of 100 pence
Languages	Gaelic and English
Religion	92% Roman Catholic
Head of State	Mary McAleese
Prime Minister	John Bruton

POPULATION PROFILE

Population (1995)	3.5 million			
Labour Force (1995)	Labour force (000s)	1,424	as a percentage of population	39.8

Civilians in Employment by Sector	%		%
Agriculture, forestry, fishing	9.8	Wholesale, retail, restaurants, hotels	13.0
Mining, quarrying	0.4	Transport, storage, communications	5.3
Manufacturing	17.1		
Electricity, gas, water	0.9	Finance, insurance, real estate, business services	20.1
Construction	5.8	Public administration and defence	5.1
		Not defined	22.5

Unemployment Rate (1996) 14.6%

Population by age and sex (1995)

Age Group	Total 000s	%	Male 000s	%	Female 000s	%
0–4	259	7.2	134	3.7	126	3.5
5–9	290	8.1	148	4.1	141	3.9
10–14	337	9.4	173	4.8	164	4.6
15–24	613	17.1	313	8.7	300	8.4
25–34	502	14.0	247	6.9	255	7.1
35–44	483	13.5	240	6.7	243	6.8
45–54	397	11.1	201	5.6	196	5.5
55–64	287	8.0	143	4.0	144	4.0
65+	412	11.5	176	4.9	236	6.6
Total	**3,580**	**100.0**	**1,776**	**49.6**	**1,804**	**50.4**

Population per sq. km. 50.9

ECONOMIC PROFILE

GNP per capita, IR£ billion (1995)	33.8				

5 biggest companies (1995)

Rank	Company	Sector	Turnover IR£ million	No. of Employees
1	Jefferson Smurfitt Group	Print & packaging	1,710	19,354
2	CRH	Building materials	1,613	13,691
3	Aer Lingus	Air transportation	1,481	11,370
4	Intel Ireland	Computer manuf.	1,200	2,800
5	Avonmore Foods	Dairy/pigmeat processor	1,191	6,219

Value of exports FOB, US$ bn (1995) 44.0

Value of imports CIF, US$ bn (1995) 32.6

Central bank Central Bank

POLITICAL PROFILE

Constitution/ electoral system	*Dáil Éireann* (house of representatives – lower house) has 166 members elected every 5 years. *Seanad Éireann* (senate) has 60 members; 11 nominated by the Prime Minister, 6 elected by universities, 43 elected from panels of candidates.
Local government	Local authorities are elected every 5 years. All local authorities have a dual management system being jointly run by elected representatives and paid offices.
Last election	June 1997
Results	Fianna Fail 77 Fine Gael 54 Labour 17 Others 10 Progressive Democrats 4 Democratic Left 4

INTERNATIONAL RELATIONS

Ireland is a member of:	UN, OECD, Council of Europe, EU.

TRANSPORT INFRASTRUCTURE

Rail	1,872 km. in 1995.
Road	939,022 private cars in 1994.
Air	Aer Lingus. Principal airports at Dublin, Shannon and Cork.

COMMUNICATIONS

Newspapers	7 daily newspapers with a total circulation of 647,912.
TV/Radio	RTE provides public service broadcasting. 21 local commercial radio stations.

Italy

Land Area	301,046 sq. km.
Capital	Rome
Currency	Lira
Languages	Italian
Religion	100% Roman Catholic
Head of State (President)	Oscar Luigi Scalfaro
Prime Minister	Romano Prodi

POPULATION PROFILE

Population (1995)	57.2 million

Labour Force (1994)

Labour force (000s)	23,210		as a percentage of population	40.6

Civilians in Employment by Sector

	%		%
Agriculture, forestry, fishing	7.9	Wholesale, retail, restaurants, hotels	21.1
Mining & Manufacturing	22.7	Transport, storage, communications	5.4
Electricity, gas, water	1.5	Finance, insurance, real estate, business services	7.6
Construction	8.2	Public administration and defence	25.7

Unemployment Rate (1996)

12.1%

Population by age and sex (1995)

Age Group	Total 000s	Total %	Male 000s	Male %	Female 000s	Female %
0–4	2,770	4.8	1,422	2.5	1,348	2.4
5–9	2,795	4.9	1,431	2.5	1,364	2.4
10–14	3,056	5.3	1,562	2.7	1,494	2.6
15–24	8,139	14.2	4,146	7.2	3,993	7.0
25–34	9,189	16.0	4,628	8.1	4,561	8.0
35–44	7,738	13.5	3,859	6.7	3,879	6.8
45–54	7,338	12.8	3,620	6.3	3,717	6.5
55–64	6,844	12.0	3,275	5.7	3,569	6.2
65+	9,401	16.4	3,848	6.7	5,553	9.7
Total	**57,269**	**100.0**	**27,791**	**48.4**	**29,478**	**51.6**

Population per sq. km.

190.1

ECONOMIC PROFILE

GNP per capita, Lira trillion (1994)	1,559

Rank	Company	Sector	Turnover Lira billion	No. of Employees
1	ENEL	Petroleum, oil	33,365	101,849
2	Telecom Italia	Telecommunication	29,158	97,815
3	Fiat Auto	Automotive	23,393	74,499
4	Agip Petrol	Petroleum, oil	17,602	10,771
5	Snam	Petroleum, oil	12,262	6,317

5 biggest companies (1994)

Value of exports FOB, US$ bn (1995)	234
Value of imports CIF, US$ bn (1995)	206
Central bank	Bank of Italy

POLITICAL PROFILE

Constitution/ electoral system	Republic. Chamber of Deputies (lower house) has 630 members elected every 5 years. Senate (upper house) has 315 elected senators elected by the regions.
Local government	15 autonomous regions, plus 5 regions with special autonomy. Each has its own parliament (*consiglio regionale*) and government (*giunta regionale and presidente*). The powers wielded by these authorities vary from one region to another.
Last election	April 1996
Results	Olive Tree Alliance 284 Freedom Alliance (Forza Italia, National Alliance, Christian Democratic Centre) 246 Northern League 59 Communist Refoundation Party 35 Others 6

INTERNATIONAL RELATIONS

Italy is a member of:	UN, NATO, EU, WEU and the Schengen Accord.

TRANSPORT INFRASTRUCTURE

Rail	19,595 km. in 1991.
Road	303,518 km. in 1991. 27,415,828 cars registered in 1990.
Air	Alitalia. 9 international airports.

COMMUNICATIONS

Newspapers	73 daily newspapers in 1988 with a circulation of 6 million.
TV/Radio	12 national and 820 local independent TV networks. 3 national radio programmes (in addition to regional programmes).

Luxembourg

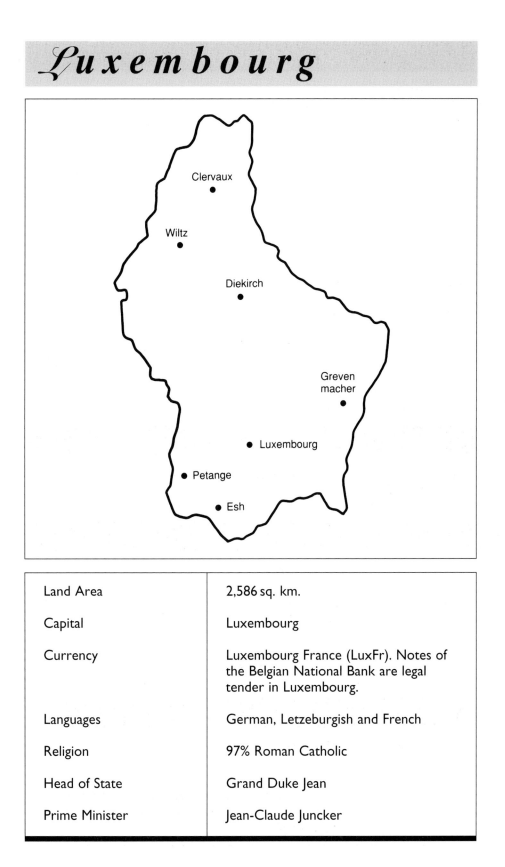

Land Area	2,586 sq. km.
Capital	Luxembourg
Currency	Luxembourg France (LuxFr). Notes of the Belgian National Bank are legal tender in Luxembourg.
Languages	German, Letzeburgish and French
Religion	97% Roman Catholic
Head of State	Grand Duke Jean
Prime Minister	Jean-Claude Juncker

POPULATION PROFILE

Population (1996)	412,800

Labour Force (1995)

Labour force (000s)	171.1	as a percentage of population	42.1

Civilians in Employment by Sector

	%		%
Agriculture, forestry	2.7	Construction	10.8
Mining, quarrying, manufacturing	15.7	Market Services	55.2
Electricity, gas, water	0.7	Non-market services	14.9

Unemployment Rate (1996) 3.1%

Population by age and sex (1996)

Age Group	Total 000s	%	Male 000s	%	Female 000s	%
0–4	27,560	6.7	14,144	3.4	13,416	3.3
5–9	25,627	6.2	13,108	3.2	12,519	3.0
10–14	23,086	5.6	11,892	2.9	11,194	2.7
15–24	48,350	11.7	24,508	5.9	23,842	5.8
25–34	69,570	16.9	35,346	8.6	34,224	8.3
35–44	65,508	15.9	33,348	8.1	32,160	7.8
45–54	52,055	12.6	26,911	6.5	25,144	6.1
55–64	42,884	10.4	20,999	5.1	21,885	5.3
65+	58,160	14.1	22,344	5.4	35,816	8.7
Total	**412,800**	**100.0**	**202,600**	**49.1**	**210,200**	**50.9**

Population per sq. km. 159.6

ECONOMIC PROFILE

GNP per capita, LFr billion (1993)	500.4

5 biggest companies (1994)

Rank	Company	Sector	No. of Employees
1	Arbed	Steel	7,340
2	Goodyear	Tyres	3,480
3	CFL Luxembourg	Transport	3,290
4	P et T	Post Office	2,560
5	Groupe Cactus	Food/restaurants	2,420

Value of exports FOB, US$ bn (1995)	169.2
Value of imports CIF, US$ bn (1995)	154.8
Central bank	Monetary Institute

POLITICAL PROFILE

Constitution/ electoral system	Constitutional monarchy. Chamber of Deputies (lower house) bas 60 members, elected every 5 years. Council of State (upper house) has 21 members chosen for life by the sovereign.
Local government	Because of its small size, there are no rigid divisions between central and local government. There are 4 electoral districts.
Last election	June 1994
Results	Christian Social Party (CS) 21 Socialist Workers' Party (S) 17 Democratic Party 12 Action Committee for Democracy 5 Déi-Gréng GLEI-GAP 5

INTERNATIONAL RELATIONS

Luxembourg is a member of:	UN, EU, OECD, the Council of Europe, NATO, WEU and the Schengen Accord.

TRANSPORT INFRASTRUCTURE

Rail	275 km. in 1994.
Road	5,136 km. in 1995. 229,037 cars registered in 1995.
Air	Luxair is the national airline. 1 international airport.

COMMUNICATIONS

Newspapers	5 daily newspapers with a combined circulation of 154,000.
TV/Radio	Compagnie Luxembourgeoise de Télédiffusion.

The Netherlands

Land Area	4,160 sq. km.
Capital	Amsterdam (seat of government The Hague)
Currency	Guilder (Fl) of 100 cents
Languages	Dutch
Religion	36% Roman Catholic 27% Protestant 4% Others 33% Unaffiliated
Head of State	Queen Beatrix
Prime Minister	Wim Kok

POPULATION PROFILE

Population (1996)

15.4 million

Labour Force (1994)

| Labour force (000s) | 7,184 | as a percentage of population | 46.7 |

Civilians in Employment by Sector	%		%
Agriculture, forestry, fishing	3.9	Wholesale retail, restaurants, hotels	18.3
Mining, quarrying	0.1	Transport, storage, communications	6.3
Manufacturing	16.1		
Electricity, gas, water	0.7	Finance, insurance, real estate, business services	10.5
Construction	5.9	Community, social, personal services	35.4
		Not defined	2.8

Unemployment Rate (1996)

7.0%

Population by age and sex (1996)

Age Group	Total 000s	%	Male 000s	%	Female 000s	%
0–4	981	6.3	502	3.2	479	3.1
5–9	964	6.2	493	3.2	471	3.0
10–14	903	5.8	461	3.0	442	2.9
15–24	2,004	12.9	1,020	6.6	984	6.3
25–34	2,620	16.9	1,340	8.7	1,280	8.3
35–44	2,391	15.4	1,215	7.8	1,176	7.6
45–54	2,102	13.6	1,074	6.9	1,029	6.6
55–64	1,468	9.5	728	4.7	740	4.8
65+	2,061	13.3	829	5.3	1,232	8.0
Total	**15,494**	**100.0**	**7,662**	**49.5**	**7,832**	**50.5**

Population per sq. km.

456

ECONOMIC PROFILE

GNP per capita, Fl thousand (1994)

39.1

5 biggest companies (1995)

Rank	Company	Sector	Turnover Fl million	No. of Employees
1	Shell Group	Chemicals, oils	176,771	104,000
2	Unilever	Conglomerate	79,703	308,000
3	Phillips Electrical	Electronics	64,462	263,554
4	Ahold	Retail	29,617	84,438
5	SHV Holdings	Industry	25,963	46,233

Value of exports FOB, US$ bn (1994)

155.0

Value of imports CIF, US$ bn (1994)

139.8

Central bank

Netherlands Bank

POLITICAL PROFILE

Constitution/ electoral system	Constitutional monarchy. Second Chamber has 150 deputies elected every 4 years. Upper or First Chamber has 75 members elected indirectly by provincial councils.
Local government	12 provinces consisting of 636 municipalities.
Last election	May 1994
Results	Labour Party (PvdA) .... 37 Christian Democratic Alliance (CDA) ... 34 Liberals (VVD) .... 31 Democrats '66 .... 24 General Association for the Elderly ... 6 Green Left (Grl) .... 5 Evangelical Political Federation (RPF) ... 3 Centre Democrats (CD) .... 3 Calvinist Party (SGD) .... 2 Reformed Political League (GPV) ... 2 Socialist Party (SP) .... 2 Union 55+ 1

INTERNATIONAL RELATIONS

The Netherlands is a member of:	UN, EU, OECD, Council of Europe, WEU, NATO and the Schengen Accord.

TRANSPORT INFRASTRUCTURE

Rail	NV Nederlandse Spoorwegen runs the railways. 2,757 km. in 1994.
Road	56,030 km. in 1992. Number of private cars: 5.6 million in 1995.
Air	KLM national airline. 4 international airports.

COMMUNICATIONS	
Newspapers	9 daily and 2 weekly newspapers in 1995.
TV/Radio	3 national TV channels. 5 national radio stations.

Portugal

Land Area	92,100 sq. km.
Capital	Lisbon
Currency	Escudo (Es) of 100 centavos
Languages	Portuguese
Religion	95% Roman Catholic
Head of State	Jorge Sampaio
Prime Minister	Antonio Guterres

POPULATION PROFILE

Population (1996)

9.9 million

Labour Force (1993)

Labour force (000s)	4,772	as a percentage of population	48.3

Civilians in Employment by Sector

	%		%
Agriculture, forestry, fishing	11.3	Wholesale, retail, restaurants, hotels	19.4
Mining quarrying	0.5	Transport, storage, communications	4.7
Manufacturing	23.8		
		Finance, insurance, business services	6.9
Electricity, gas, water	0.7		
		Community, social, personal services	24.6
Construction	8.1		

Unemployment Rate (1996)

7.6%

Population by age and sex (1996)

Age Group	Total 000s	%	Male 000s	%	Female 000s	%
0–4	556	5.6	286	2.9	270	2.7
5–9	544	5.5	278	2.8	266	2.7
10–14	645	6.5	330	3.3	315	3.2
15–24	1,620	16.3	819	8.3	801	8.1
25–34	1,489	15.0	742	7.5	748	7.5
35–44	1,348	13.6	657	6.6	691	7.0
45–54	1,186	12.0	568	5.7	618	6.2
55–64	1,077	10.9	500	5.0	577	5.8
65+	1,457	14.7	600	6.0	856	8.6
Total	**9,921**	**100.0**	**4,778**	**48.2**	**5,143**	**51.8**

Population per sq. km.

108

ECONOMIC PROFILE

GNP per capita, Es billion (1993)	12,476			

5 biggest companies (1995)	Rank	Company	Sector	Turnover Es million	No. of Employees
	1	Petróleos de Portugal	Petroleum	768,153	3,622
	2	Portugal Telecom	Telecom-munications	387,445	19,584
	3	Rede Eléctrica Nacional	Energy	290,939	796
	4	Electricidade do Norte	Energy	225,882	4,463
	5	Pâo de Açúcar	Food retail	224,379	–

Value of exports FOB, US$ bn (1995)	22.8
Value of imports CIF, US$ bn (1995)	32.5
Central bank	Banco de Portugal

POLITICAL PROFILE

Constitution/ electoral system	Republic. Assembly of the Republic has 230 deputies elected every 4 years.
Local government	18 districts consisting of 305 municipal authorities and 4,209 parishes. Assemblies are directly elected at each level. The Azores and Madeira are autonomous regions, also with directly elected assemblies.
Last election	October 1995
Results	Socialist Party 112 Social Democratic Party 88 Christian Democratic Party 15 Communist Alliance 15

INTERNATIONAL RELATIONS

Portugal is a member of:	UN, EU, OECD, NATO, WEU, Council of Europe and the Schengen Accord.

TRANSPORT INFRASTRUCTURE

Rail	3,072 km. in 1994.
Road	9,648 km. of national roads in 1993. 4,360,447 vehicles registered in 1993.
Air	TAP-Air Portugal is the national carrier. 5 international airports.

COMMUNICATIONS

Newspapers	27 dailies in 1994 with a circulation of 137,301,00.
TV/Radio	2 state owned TV channels 2 independent TV channels. Radiodifusão Portuguesa broadcasts national and regional radio programmes.

Spain

Land Area	504,800 sq. km.
Capital	Madrid
Currency	Peseta (Pta)
Languages	Spanish, Castilian, Catalan, Galician and Basque
Religion	99% Roman Catholic
Head of State	King Juan Carlos
Prime Minister	Jose Maria Aznar

POPULATION PROFILE

Population (1995)

39.2 million

Labour Force (1993)

| Labour force (000s) | 15,564 | as a percentage of population | 39.8 |

Civilians in Employment by Sector	%		%
Agriculture, forestry, fishing	10.1	Wholesale, retail, restaurants, hotels	21
Mining, quarrying	0.5	Transport, storage, communications	5.9
Manufacturing	20.3		
		Finance, insurance, real estate, business services	6.5
Electricity, gas, water	0.7		
Construction	9.2	Community, social, personal services	25.7
		Not defined	0.1

Unemployment Rate (1996)

22.1%

Population by age and sex (1995)

Age Group	Total 000s	%	Male 000s	%	Female 000s	%
0–4	1,934	4.9	998	2.5	936	2.4
5–9	2,055	5.2	1,055	2.7	1,000	2.6
10–14	2,529	6.5	1,296	3.3	1,233	3.1
15–24	6,454	16.5	3,298	8.4	3,156	8.0
25–24	6,314	16.1	3,196	8.2	3,118	8.0
35–44	5,296	13.5	2,649	6.8	2,648	6.8
45–54	4,514	11.5	2,234	5.7	2,280	5.8
55–64	4,125	10.5	1,977	5.0	2,148	5.5
65+	5,988	15.3	2,488	6.3	3,500	8.9
Total	**39,210**	**100.0**	**19,191**	**48.9**	**20,019**	**51.1**

Population per sq. km.

80.2

ECONOMIC PROFILE

	Rank	Company	Sector	Market Capital Pta million
GNP per capita, Pta billion (1994)		63.5		
5 biggest companies (1996)	1	Telefonica	Communications	2,001,072
	2	Endesa	Electricity & Gas	1,898,040
	3	Repsol	Petroleum	1,263,000
	4	Banco Bilbao-Vizcaya	Banking	1,197,810
	5	Iberdrola	Electricity	1,053,896
Value of exports FOB, US$ bn (1995)		91.6		
Value of imports CIF, US$ bn (1995)		114.8		
Central bank		Bank of Spain		

POLITICAL PROFILE

Constitution/ electoral system	Constitutional monarchy. Congress of Deputies (lower house) has 350 members elected every 4 years. Senate (upper house) has 252 members elected by the provinces.
Local government	A semi-federal system of regional administration with 17 autonomous communities, each with an elected parliament and a regional government exercising legislative and executive powers in certain areas. Communities break down into 50 provinces made up of 8,077 municipalities.
Last election	March 1996
Results	Popular Party (PP) 156 Socialists (PSOE) 141 United Left (IU) 21 Convergencia I Unio (CIU) 16 EAJ-PNV 5 CC 4 BNG 2 HB 2 ERC 1 EA-EUE 1 UV 1

INTERNATIONAL RELATIONS

Spain is a member of:	UN, Council of Europe, NATO, WEU, EU, OECD and the Schengen Accord.

TRANSPORT INFRASTRUCTURE

Rail	14,589 km. in 1994.
Road	160,136 km. in 1993.
Air	Iberia Airlines is the national carrier. 17 international airports.

COMMUNICATIONS	
Newspapers	90 daily newspapers in 1994 with a circulation of 4 million.
TV/Radio	Public radio has 5 national and many regional radio networks. There are 2 independent radio networks. 2 national TV networks. 8 regional TV programmes. 3 nationwide commercial TV networks.

Sweden

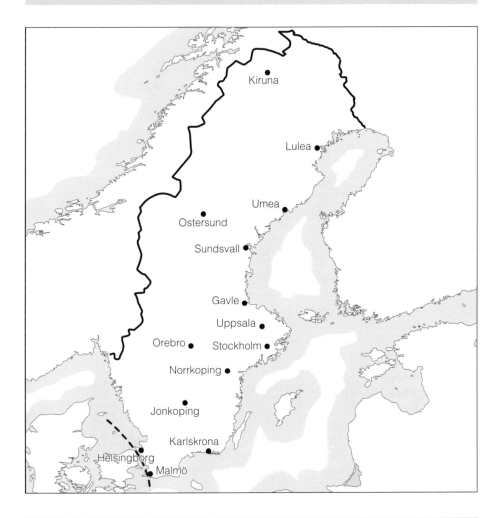

Land Area	410,930 sq. km.
Capital	Stockholm
Currency	Swedish Kroner (SKr)
Languages	Swedish
Religion	Evangelical Lutheran
Head of State	Carl XVI Gustaf
Prime Minister	Göran Persson

POPULATION PROFILE

Population (1996)	8.8 million

Labour Force (1994)

Labour force (000s)	4,266	as a percentage of population	77.6

Civilians in Employment by Sector

Sector	%	Sector	%
Agriculture, forestry	3.4	Wholesale, retail, restaurants, hotels	14.5
Mining, quarrying	0.2		
		Transport, storage, communications	6.9
Manufacturing	18.3		
Electricity, gas, water	0.8	Finance, insurance, business services	9.6
Construction	5.6	Community, social, personal services	40.5
		Not defined	0.2

Unemployment Rate (1996) 10.1%

Population by age and sex (1996)

Age Group	Total 000s	Total %	Male 000s	Male %	Female 000s	Female %
0–4	582	6.6	299	3.4	284	3.2
5–9	581	6.6	298	3.4	283	3.2
10–14	502	5.7	258	2.9	244	2.8
15–24	1,087	12.3	555	6.3	532	6.0
25–34	1,252	14.2	641	7.3	610	6.9
35–44	1,174	13.3	599	6.8	576	6.5
45–54	1,256	14.2	638	7.2	618	7.0
55–64	860	9.7	425	4.8	435	4.9
65+	1,543	17.5	653	7.4	891	10.1
Total	**8,838**	**100.0**	**4,366**	**49.4**	**4,472**	**50.6**

Population per sq. km. 21.5

ECONOMIC PROFILE

GNP per capita, SKr billion (1993)	1,400

5 biggest companies (1995)

Rank	Company	Sector	Turnover SKr million	No. of Employees
1	ABB	Electrical equip.	239,877	209,637
2	Volvo	Automotive	171,511	80,369
3	Electrolux	Household durables	115,800	112,300
4	Ericsson	Communications	98,780	80,338
5	Tetral Laval	Industrial suppliers	70,200	44,300

Value of exports FOB, US$ bn (1995)	79.1

Value of imports CIF, US$ bn (1995)	64.3

Central bank	Sveriges Riksbank

POLITICAL PROFILE

Constitution/ electoral system	Parliamentary democracy. Single Chamber (*Riksdag*) of 349 members elected for 4 years.
Local government	24 counties each with a governor appointed by the government. 14 other members elected by the county council.
Last election	September 1994
Results	Social Democratic Party 162 Moderate Party 80 Centre Party 27 Liberal Party 26 Left Party 22 Green Party 18 Christian Democratic Party 14

INTERNATIONAL RELATIONS

Sweden is a member of:	UN, EU, NATO and the Partnership for Peace.

TRANSPORT INFRASTRUCTURE

Rail	10,798 km. in 1994.
Road	0.21 km. public roads in 1995.
Air	SAS. 2 international airports.

COMMUNICATIONS

Newspapers	174 daily newspapers in 1995.
TV/Radio	2 TV programmes. 3 commercial satellite channels. 3 national and regional radio programmes.

U K

Land Area	24,111 sq. km.
Capital	London
Currency	Pound Sterling (£) of 100 pence
Languages	English
Religion	71% Protestant 13% Roman Catholic 16% Other or unaffiliated
Head of State	Queen Elizabeth II
Prime Minister	Tony Blair

POPULATION PROFILE

Population (1995)	58.6 million			
Labour Force (1996)	Unemployment	2,097	as a percentage of workforce	7.5
	Labour force (000s)	27,920	as a percentage of population	47.6

Civilians in Employment by Sector

	%		%
Agriculture, forestry, fishing	1.4	Hotels and restaurants	6.0
Electricity, gas and water supply	1.0	Transport and communications	5.9
Mining and quarrying	0.3	Financial, real estate, business	17.0
Manufacturing	17.7	Public administration, defence and social security	6.1
Construction	3.8		
Wholesale, retail, trade and repairs	16.7	Education	8.4
		Health, social work and other services	15.9

Unemployment Rate (1996): 8.4%

Population by age and sex (1995)

Age Group	Total 000s	%	Male 000s	%	Female 000s	%
0–4	3,836	6.5	1,965	3.4	1,871	3.2
5–9	3,860	6.6	1,980	3.4	1,880	3.2
10–14	3,666	6.3	1,882	3.2	1,785	3.0
15–24	7,450	12.7	3,825	6.5	3,625	6.2
25–34	9,409	16.1	4,794	8.2	4,616	7.9
35–44	7,931	13.5	3,984	6.8	3,947	6.7
45–54	7,435	12.7	3,711	6.3	3,724	6.4
55–64	5,795	9.9	2,848	4.9	2,947	5.0
65+	9,225	15.7	3,740	6.4	5,485	9.4
Total	**58,606**	**100.0**	**28,728**	**49.0**	**29,878**	**51.0**

Population per sq. km.: 240.1

ECONOMIC PROFILE

GNP per capita, £ billion (1995)

710.5

5 biggest companies (1995)

Rank	Company	Sector	Turnover £ million	No. of Employees
1	British Petroleum	Oil	33,116	66,550
2	Shell Transport & Trading	Oil	24,772	–
3	HSBC Holdings	Banking	13,975	106,861
4	British Telecom	Telecommunications	13,893	148,900
5	Barclays	Banking	13,429	95,700

Value of exports FOB, US$ bn (1995)

242.6

Value of imports CIF, US$ bn (1995)

265.7

Central bank

Bank of England

POLITICAL PROFILE

Constitution/ electoral system	Constitutional monarchy. House of Commons (lower house) has 651 members elected every 5 years. House of Lords (upper house) has 1,184 members including hereditary and life peers appointed by the sovereign.

Local government	Elected councils carry out administration of local government.
	Different systems exist in England, Wales and Scotland.
	Single-tier unitary authorities have recently been set up.
	1997: 35 (2 tier) non-metropolitan county councils
	          274 district councils
	           27 (1 tier) unitary authorities
	           36 metropolitan district councils
	           32 Greater London borough councils

Last election	May 1997
Results	Labour 418 Conservative 165 Liberal Democrats 46 Ulster Unionists 9 Plaid Cymru 4 SDLP 2 DUP 6 Others 1

INTERNATIONAL RELATIONS

UK is a member of:	UN, Commonwealth, EU, OECD, Council of Europe, WEU and NATO.

TRANSPORT INFRASTRUCTURE

Rail	16,542 km. in 1995.
Road	20,505,000 private cars in 1995.
Air	British Airways. 17 major airports including 2 major international airports at Gatwick and Heathrow.

COMMUNICATIONS

Newspapers	10 national dailies in 1994 with a combined circulation of 13.2 million.
TV/Radio	Public service broadcasting provided by the BBC (television and radio). 3 major independent commercial channels. A wide network of national, local and commercial radio stations.

Country Profiles ... What Next?

The European Union is likely to be enlarged early in the twenty-first century. Students may wish to consider:

- Which countries are most likely to become the newest members of the European Union?
- Which countries currently hold associate member status?
- Is there an optimum size for the European Union?
- How will the current member states treat the former Eastern-bloc countries?

2 *Living and Working in Europe*

This chapter covers:
★ The development and provisions of the Social Charter
★ The difference between the Social Charter and the Social Chapter
★ A summary of EU social policy in four areas: work, social protection, health and education
★ A review of social provision in each of these four areas for each member state

Introduction

The opening up of Europe by the Single European Act of 1986, in particular with the coming into effect of the Single Market on 1 January 1993, has provided new opportunities for all its citizens to sample life in member states other than their own. It is now much easier not only to travel around Europe as a visitor, but also to live and work in other EU countries.

It is therefore important to be aware of the factors affecting life both within and outside the workplace in the various states – the more so because, as this chapter will show, these factors vary enormously from one country to another.

To enable comparisons between countries, the latter part of this chapter is divided, like Chapter 1, into sections dealing with the individual states. Each section sets out the provisions in that country relating to:

- working conditions
- social protection
- health
- education

However, national provisions are only part of the story. The Union itself has, since its inception, taken a strong interest in the development of living and working conditions for all its citizens, and this – now commonly referred to as Union 'social policy' – has been, and continues to be, a prominent and controversial policy area.

Social Charter and Social Chapter

Central to Union policy on living and working conditions is the Union Charter of Fundamental Social Rights for Workers (the 'Social Charter') signed by eleven of the then twelve member states – not the UK – in December 1989. These principles were further enshrined in the Social Chapter of the Maastricht Treaty, which again met with strong resistance from Britain. Tony Blair's Labour government elected in May 1997, however, has committed itself to signing the Social Charter.

The Social Charter grew out of the conviction held by many of those in the policy-making circles of the Union, that the protection of workers is vital to the economic progress and development of the EU. Not all Europe's workers were adequately protected already: of the 128 million-strong European workforce, 8 million are self-employed, and 40 per cent of all employment is provided by small and medium-sized enterprises which often lack either the means or the will to effectively protect their own employees.

THE SOCIAL CHARTER

The fundamental rights covered in the Charter are as follows:

Freedom of movement
Every worker in the EU is free to move about the EU, to take up any occupation or profession in an EU country, and to be treated in the same way as a national of that country in terms of access to employment, working conditions and social protection.

Employment and remuneration
Every worker may work in whichever occupation field s/he chooses, providing s/he has the appropriate and relevant qualifications and satisfies any rules which govern that occupation. Each worker is also entitled to fair pay for that occupation.

Improvement of living and working conditions
It is a continuing aim of the Community to develop legislation to ensure that each worker gets a fair deal in terms of paid annual leave, weekly rest periods, redundancy provision etc. Conditions should be laid out in a worker's contract of employment.

Social protection
Every worker has the right to an adequate level of social protection with the appropriate social security benefits. This right also applies to those who are not in employment.

Freedom of association and collective bargaining
Workers are entitled to join trade unions and employers are free to form professional organisations to protect their own interests. Both workers and employers have the right not to join any organisation. Collective agreements can be negotiated by unions and professional organisations in line with national legislation and practice. The right to strike is subject to any obligation laid down in national regulations and collective agreements.

Vocational training
Every worker should have access to vocational training during his/her working life.

Equal treatment for men and women
People of both sexes should be given equal opportunity and treatment in respect of employment, education and training.

Information, consultation and participation for workers
All organisations should have a system of information, consultation and participation for its workforce. This is particularly important where a company operates in more than one member state.

Health, protection and safety in the workplace
Every worker is entitled to satisfactory health and safety conditions in the workplace.

Protection of children and young people
The minimum age of employment should not be lower than 15 or the minimum school leaving age. Under-18s should not do any nightwork. Young people should receive a fair rate of pay and are entitled to initial vocational training.

Elderly people
Every retired worker should have a decent standard of living. Those without a pension should receive adequate resources as well as medical and social assistance.

Disabled people
The disabled are entitled to be integrated socially and professionally. They should enjoy adequate provision in transport, training and housing.

The Social Charter and Social Chapter are often confused. The Social Charter is not legally binding, but is a declaration of intent by its signatories. It is supported by an action programme containing almost 50 proposals for directives and regulations, many of which are in the process of being adopted.

The Social Chapter was agreed by the same 11 member states which signed the Social Charter. It is also known as the Agreement on Social Policy and formed an annexe to the Maastricht Treaty. It is called the Social Chapter as it was meant to succeed the chapter in the Treaty of Rome on social policy – this could not happen though, as not all member states agreed to sign it. The most recent member states of Austria, Finland and Sweden have agreed to be bound by the Social Chapter.

The Social Chapter has been incorporated into the Treaty of Amsterdam and is likely to be renamed the Social Agreement.

In February 1988 the Commission published a paper on the development of the Community's social policy, highlighting the need for intensified dialogue between social partners on social policy issues. This came to be commonly known as the 'Social Dialogue'.

The most prominent advocate of a strengthened common social policy has been Jacques Delors. He has contended that the Single Market brought into being by the Single European Act should benefit individuals living and working in the EU as much as business organisations; that is, that the Act should set in motion social as well as economic reform. He declared that the Act should contain a 'social dimension' which would cover the whole area of social policy and the free movement of labour.

> The social dimension permeates all our discussions and everything we do: our efforts to restore competitiveness and cooperate on macroeconomic policy to reduce unemployment and provide all young Europeans with a working future; common policies designed to promote the development of less-prosperous regions and the regeneration of regions hit by industrial change; employment policy and the concentration of efforts on helping young people to gain a foothold in the labour market and combating long-term unemployment; and the development of rural regions threatened by the decline in the number of farms, desertification and demographic imbalances.
>
> Think what a boost it would be for democracy and social injustice if we could demonstrate that we are capable of working together to create a better integrated society open to all.
>
> Three controversial issues need to be cleared up in this context:
>
> First, the Charter of Social Rights. Its sole object is to provide a formal reminder that the Community has no intention of sacrificing fundamental workers' rights on the altar of economic efficiency. How could anyone dispute the political and rhetorical significance of this message for a people's Europe, for the man in the street? When it comes to translating these principles into legislation or collective bargaining, subsidiarity comes into its own, ensuring that our different traditions are respected. This is borne out by the Commission's social programme, which will be implemented within the bounds of the Treaty as it now stands.

Jacques Delors, Bruges, 17 October 1989

The Maastricht Treaty

Many members of the EU demonstrated a will to speed up social legislation when they agreed to the Social Chapter of the Maastricht Treaty. The mechanism for facilitating this was to use qualified majority voting for certain policy areas which previously would have required unanimous approval. Areas falling within this remit include health and safety, working conditions, equal opportunities and consultation of the workforce. Unanimous agreement is still required concerning key areas such as social protection and collective agreement.

Attitudes to the social dimension are reflected in the following Eurobarometer results.

The Social Dimension of the Single Market

Most Europeans (65%) see the social dimension of the single market as a 'good thing'. Support for at least a minimum of social regulation at Community level is particularly strong in Italy (77%), Portugal (74%) and the Netherlands (73%), while the people of Luxembourg (54%), Denmark (55%) and the United Kingdom (57%) attach less importance to this kind of legislation. In Ireland 72% of people are in favour of Community rules in the social field, in Greece 71%, in Spain 70%, in Germany 63% and in Belgium and France 58%.

Source: *Eurobarometer, No. 36*, December 1991: European Commission

Social Policy in Europe: A Review

Before turning to a country-by-country analysis of work and social provision, it is worthwhile briefly reviewing the state of affairs across the EU as a whole in the four main areas addressed in this chapter: work, social protection, health and education.

Work

Levels of employment and working conditions vary considerably across the EU. Despite moves to harmonise working conditions through the Social Charter (see above) and the Social Chapter of the Maastricht Treaty, there remain differences that are difficult to eliminate, particularly in view of the different rates at which member states' economies are developing. Working conditions also vary according to national custom and practice, cultural conditions and attitudes towards work, and political objectives.

Understandably, during a period of world recession in the early 1990s, unemployment is a major concern for most European countries. In 1993 there were 16.3 million unemployed in the Community (10 per cent of the active population).

Source: *Eurostat Yearbook 1995*

Social Protection

The degree of commitment to social protection and the benefits provided to citizens vary widely among the member states (see following table).

Different Social Situations

	Employment (1991)				Net hourly earnings in industry (1991) ECU	Social protection benefits (1990)	
	Total	Agriculture (%)	Industry (%)	Services (%)		% of GDP	ECU per inhabitant
B	3,758	2.6	27.7	69.6	8.63	26.8[3]	3,517[3]
DK	2,650	5.4	26.0	68.6	12.47	28.8	5,613
D[1]	28,886	3.2	38.6	58.2	10.65	26.9	4,386
GR	3,643	21.6	25.0	53.4	3.67	16.9[3]	710
E	12,916	10.4	32.3	57.3	6.54	17.8	1,690
F	22,322	5.6	28.8	65.6	6.77	28.0	4.401
IRL	1,125	13.7	28.6	57.6	7.40	20.6	1,876
I	21,946	8.3	31.5	60.2	7.62	23.6	3,350
L	197	3.0	29.9	66.5	8.37[2]	26.7	4,619
NL	6,521	4.5	25.2	70.3	8.71	31.2	4,393
P	4,898	17.3	33.3	49.4	2.10	17.0	7.58
UK	26,049	2.1	27.6	68.9	8.33	20.7[3]	2,627[3]
EC	**134,911**	**6.1**	**31.2**	**62.4**		**24.6[3]**	**3,183[3]**

1   Federal Republic of Germany as constituted prior to 3.0.1990
2   1990
3   1980

Source: Eurostat

Expenditure on social protection tends to be raised from three main sources: contributions from employers, contributions from employees and public funds. Each country applies a unique blend of these sources.

Health

The Union's citizens by and large enjoy good health supported by well-developed health services. Subject to neither extremes of climate not extremes of general poverty, Europe escapes many of the severe health problems suffered in harsher and poorer regions of the world. There are, however, areas of concern that all 15 member states have to confront, although their methods and structures of health provision vary widely.

Life expectancy continues to grow. In 1991 life expectancy at birth stood at 79.8 for girls and 72.9 for boys with decreasing infant mortality. Major causes of death continue to be heart disease, respiratory illness, cancer and road traffic accidents.

Education

The declining birth rate in Europe has inevitably impacted school rolls. However, education continues to play an important part in citizens' lives in the 15 EU member states.

It is evident from studying each of the member states' systems that common themes emerge: the increase of students within the tertiary sector, the strength of female educational participation at all levels, confirming equal opportunity measures and the focus on education to provide a trained, skilled workforce which will inevitably support the economic development of the member states.

Working Life – The National Provisions

AUSTRIA

Working Week	36–40 hours
Public Holidays	13 or 14 depending on religion of employee
Paid Holidays	30–36 days per year dependent on length of service
Minimum Wage	Not stipulated by law, but may be by collective agreement
Sick Pay	Full pay for 6 months, 50% thereafter
Maternity Leave	8 weeks before and 8 weeks after the birth mothers may not work. Mothers or fathers are entitled to maternity leave until the child's 2nd birthday
Termination	Employee gives 1 month, employer 6 weeks–5 months depending on length of service.

Social Protection

- Austria enjoys a comprehensive system of social security and welfare covering medical care, pensions, unemployment benefit, family allowances, etc.
- This system centres on a compulsory insurance scheme
- The retirement age is 65 for men and 60 for women and there is provision for early retirement at 60 and 55 respectively
- There is a particularly generous scheme of maternity and paternity leave

Health

- Health care in Austria covers treatment by GPs, medical rehabilitation and hospital treatment
- The majority of the services are free for most Austrian citizens, although prescription charges are levied
- Austria had 29,520 registered doctors in 1994 and 323 hospitals with 77,000 beds
- In 1992, life expectancy was 72.8 for men and 79.3 for women

Education

- 93 per cent of schools in Austria are state schools
- Education is free and compulsory between the ages of 6 and 15
- Age 6–10, pupils can attend a primary (*Grundschule* or *Volksschule*) or remedial school (*Sonderschule*)
- Age 11–14, pupils attend either a basic secondary school (*Hauptschule*), junior section of eight-year secondary school (*Unterstufte AHS*) or upper section of eight-year primary or remedial school
- Age 15 (final compulsory year of schooling), pupils attend either a polytechnic year or a vocational secondary school or continue attendance of the eight-year primary, basic secondary or remedial school
- Following the end of compulsory education, pupils have a number of choices:
  – an apprenticeship combined with part-time study
  – to continue with intermediate vocational training for 1–3 years
  – to take up teacher-training for kindergarten teachers
  – full-length secondary vocational training
  – to continue with general secondary education
- Following on, pupils can then enter tertiary education
- There are 12 universities and 6 art colleges in Austria

BELGIUM

Working Week	38 hours
Public Holidays	11
Paid Holidays	25
Minimum Wage	Fixed by collective agreement. Under 21s get a percentage of the full minimum wage
Sick Pay	52 weeks at 60% of salary
Maternity Leave	14 weeks statutory leave (8 to be taken after birth)
Termination	Blue collar, 7–56 days depending on length of service While collar: 3 months for every 5 years' service

Social Protection

- Social security contributions are made to a central department called the National Social Security Office
- Contributions are paid in part by the employee and in part by the employer; the state provides any remaining amount
- Every active citizen is obliged by law to contribute to the social security system
- Other organisations which focus on social protection issues are the *Centre Public d'Aide Social* for French-speaking parts of the country and the *Openbaar Centrum voor Maatschappelijk Welzijn* for Flemish-speaking areas. These agencies work through the local system of communes
- The major benefits are:
  – sickness and invalidity
  – insurance
  – old age and survivors' pensions
  – unemployment benefit
  – child benefit
- In 1993, Belgium spent 26.3 per cent of its GDP on social security provision

Health

- Belgium's health care system gives a high standard of care to its citizens
- Doctors' and dentists' fees and charges are largely reimbursed by social insurance
- There is one doctor and one dentist to every 300 inhabitants

- Provision for 1989/90 indicates 33,000 doctors, 7,300 dentists and 50,354 hospital beds

Education

- Education is free and compulsory for children from 6 to 18 years
- Compulsory education is the responsibility of the Flemish and Walloon communities

Pre-school

- Voluntary kindergartens and nurseries are available, but attendance is not compulsory

Primary

- Primary and infant schools number around 9,000

Secondary

- There are 2,000 middle schools which offer both general and technical classes

Tertiary

- There are 7 state and 10 private universities; student numbers total just over 100,000

DENMARK

Working Week	38 hours
Public Holidays	13
Paid Holidays	26–30
Minimum Wage	No statutory, but fixed in collective agreement for over 18s
Sick Pay	White collar: full pay Blue collar: full pay if in a collective agreement. Sickness benefit for 52 weeks
Maternity Leave	4 weeks before birth and 24 weeks after birth (last 10 weeks may be taken by the father instead). A further 2 weeks may be taken by the father. Many large employee groups receive full pay during maternity leave, otherwise maternity payments are made by the state
Termination	Blue collar: 21 days in collective agreements (but no statutory provision) White collar: 1–6 months

Social Protection

- Denmark enjoys a healthy, universal, social protection system providing free medial care, pensions, unemployment benefit, family allowances, etc.
- Social expenditure amounts to 31 per cent of GDP, which is higher than the EU average of 27 per cent
- Flexible retirement is available at the age of 60 until the retirement age of 67
- Much of the social policy is enacted by local authorities
- The system covers 3 main areas:
  – service and care functions, for example, care for the elderly
  – measures for special groups, for example, the disabled
  – transfer payments, for example, old age pensions
- In 1993 Denmark spent 32.3 per cent of its GDP on social security provision

Health

- Health care in Denmark comprises hospital services and primary health-care services
- Most of these services are free of charge (exceptions to this rule are payments for physiotherapy, drugs and dental treatment)
- Health care expenditure is 6.3 per cent of GDP (1990)
- There are 3,200 GPs and 3,400 dentists in Denmark and 30,000 hospital beds
- In 1992, life expectancy was 72.6 for men and 78 for women

Education

- Schooling between the ages of 7 and 16 is free and compulsory

Pre-school

- In 1989, 69.6 per cent of Danish 3–6-year-olds attended kindergartens or pre-school classes (*børnehaveklasse*)

Primary

- 91 per cent of all Danish children attend primary school, called *Folkeskole* (people's school)
- Starting at age 7, the *Folkeskole* lasts for 9 years; an optional 10th year may be added
- In practice, streaming does not often occur in the compulsory 9-year period, although there may be some in the 8th and 9th forms
- At the end of 9 or 10 years, pupils can sit an exam, which is not compulsory, in order to receive a final grade

Secondary

- ⅔ of *Folkeskole* pupils go on to some form of vocational or practical training; ⅓ goes on to secondary schools, of which there are 3 distinct kinds
- At the *gymnasium* (upper secondary school), students take a specialist route, focusing on, for example maths or languages; they study for 3 years and take final exams
- Alternatively, students can take a 2-year course with a final exam at the *studenterkursus* (adult, upper secondary school), or a 2-year, higher, preparatory examination course with a final exam, which prepares pupils for university or other higher education
- Vocational education and training includes apprenticeship training and covers courses in many occupational fields, e.g. commerce and trade, construction, graphics, service trades, food, agriculture, transport and communication, amongst others

Tertiary

- Tertiary education in Denmark comprises all education following the 12th year of education and is divided into short courses of further education and long courses of higher education
- There are also institutions of higher education for engineering, pharmacy, dentistry, architecture and many other professions
- Over 130 institutions offer courses of higher education

FINLAND

Working Week	40 hours
Public Holidays	11
Paid Holidays	2 weekdays per month of employment. for long-term employees there is also a week-long winter holiday
Minimum Wage	Fixed by sector agreements (legally binding). Younger workers receive a percentage of full minimum wage
Sick Pay	First 7 days at 100% of salary, then at 80% of normal earnings
Maternity Leave	10 months' leave is available with maternity allowance which is still payable if the mother returns to work early. The parental leave can be split between the mother and the father
Termination	2–6 months

Social Protection

- Finland has an enviable system of social security with 18.5 per cent of the annual budget being allocated to social expenditure
- Provision covers unemployment, accident and health insurance, and family benefits, as well as pensions
- The retirement age is 65 for both men and women, although premature retirement is common

Health

- All Finns are entitled to medical care which is generally free (although some nominal fees do exist)
- There are charges for prescriptions
- Local authorities provide health centres where GP services can be accessed. Private centres also exist which provide GP services
- Finland has 430 hospitals with 11–12 beds per thousand inhabitants
- In 1992, life expectancy was 71.7 for men and 79.4 for women

Education

- Compulsory education is free and covers the ages of 7–16
- There is also a system of voluntary pre-school education for children under the age of 7
- The system focuses on:
  – basic education for 9 years (with an optional 10th year)
  – voluntary further education in either an upper secondary school (for 3 years) or a vocational school (2–5 years)
- There are 17 universities and 4 art academies in Finland with a total population of 80,000
- Students can attend university via the upper secondary schools or via the vocational schools

FRANCE

Working Week	39 hours
Public Holidays	10
Paid Holidays	30 calendar days
Minimum Wage	Statutory minimum wage, reviewed each year. Full rate applies at 18
Sick Pay	52 weeks over a three-year period at 50% of earnings
Maternity Leave	16 or 24 weeks Family with 1 or 2 children: 6 weeks before birth, 10 weeks after Family with 3 or more children: 8 weeks before, 18 weeks after Benefit is 84% of salary tax free
Termination	1 month for up to 2 year's service. Some collective agreements give more

Social Protection

- France has a comprehensive policy covering social security
- The general scheme, which covers ⅔ of the population, is an insurance scheme funded by contributions from both employees and employers, as well as the state. It covers sickness, maternity, death, invalidity, old age, accidents at work and family benefits, paid only to those who can prove a certain level of contributions
- There is also a separate, autonomous, unemployment benefit scheme
- The insurance scheme is supplemented by an assistance scheme managed by local authorities. It is made up generally of non-contributory benefits which also cover such areas as old-age pensions
- In 1993, France spent 29.2 per cent of its GDP on social security provision

Health

- Health care in France is provided by a mixture of public and private organisations: the sickness insurance system, the social aid scheme for those without social security cover, or via the private sector
- Medical care provided by GPs is paid for by the patient who is reimbursed later. Reimbursement will typically cover around 75 per cent of the charge which the patient paid
- The cost of hospital treatment is paid directly by the state

- In 1998, there were 596,476 hospital beds and 144,071 doctors in France
- In 1992, life expectancy was 73.2 for men and 81.5 for women

Education

- Education is compulsory between the ages of 6 and 16
- Education is free at all state schools (⅘ of all schools)

Pre-school

- Classes for children aged 2–5 are often given as infant classes attached to primary schools
- Priority is given to children from social underprivileged backgrounds

Primary

- This covers ages 6–11 and comprises 3 stages: preparatory (1 year), elementary (2 years) and intermediary (2 years)
- Pupils study 3 groups of subjects: French, history, geography and civics; mathematics, science and technology; and physical education and sport, art and crafts, and music

Secondary

- At age 11, all school children move on to either a college or a *lycée*
- The college will be either a *Collège d'Enseignement Géneral (C.E.G)*, or a *Collège d'Enseignement Technique (CET)*. Both educate pupils up to age 18
- Education between the ages of 11 and 15 is split into 2 cycles: the observation stage (*cycle d'observation*) and the orientation stage (*cycle d'orientation*)
- Some pupils will enter a *lycée* instead of a *CEG* or *CET*. The *lycées* provide an education which will prepare the pupil for either the general or technical *baccalauréat* examination, taken in the final year
- There are also *lycées professionels*; vocational *lycées*, offering courses which lead to vocational certificates, e.g. the *Brevet d'Enseignement Professionel*, the *Certificat d'Aptitude Professionnelle*, and the *Baccalauréat Professionel*

Tertiary

- There are 69 universities and 3 national polytechnic institutes, as well as a number of private and Catholic universities
- Higher education is also available in over 400 schools and

institutes, including the 177 *Grandes Ecoles*. These world-famous centres of excellence are selective institutions offering technological and commercial curricula. They have been responsible for producing many members of the elite who govern France

G E R M A N Y

Working Week	38 hours
Public Holidays	10–14
Paid Holidays	Many collective agreements provide for 6 weeks or more, otherwise 24 days
Minimum Wage	No statutory minimum wage, but may be fixed by collective agreements
Sick Pay	78 weeks over a 3-year period at 80% of earnings
Maternity Leave	14–18 weeks at normal salary. Either parent can take leave up to 18 months after birth
Termination	6 weeks to 6 months

Social Protection

- Germany has a comprehensive and highly-efficient system of social protection
- Old age pension is payable at 65, but workers can retire at 63 or 60. Women may claim their pension at 60
- The social health insurance scheme offers the following benefits: medical treatment, medicines, hospital care, maternity benefit, sickness payments, accident insurance and social assistance. Old age pensions are available to wage earners and salaried employers, as well as to some of the self-employed. Family allowance and unemployment benefit are also available
- In 1993, Germany spent 29.7 per cent of its GDP on social security provision

Health

- In 1993, there were 260,000 doctors in Germany along with 2,400 hospitals providing 645,000 beds
- In 1992, life expectancy was 72.6 for men and 79.1 for women

Education

- Education is compulsory for children aged 6–15 full time and for young people aged 16–18 part time

Pre-school

- Kindergartens are not part of the state-school system, and fees are charged for attendance. Nevertheless, they are very popular: over 65 per cent of all 3–6-year-olds in Germany attend kindergartens

Primary

- Attendance is for 4–6 years at the *Grundschule*, up to age 10 or 11

Secondary

- Junior secondary schools are called *Hauptschule*; around ⅓ of primary school children go to this type of school for 5 years. Then, at the age of 15 or 16, the child can go on to take a course of vocational training until the age of 18
- Intermediate schools (*Realschule*) have a 6-year course of study which leads to a graduating certificate. This certificate allows pupils to attend a technical school (*Fachschule*), which offers vocational training at an upper-secondary level. About ⅓ of all pupils gain the intermediate certificate
- The *Gymnasium*'s period of study lasts for 9 years. This is the traditional grammar school equivalent and leads to the maturity certificate or *Arbitur*, which is vital for university entrance

Vocational education

- This is a key strength of Germany's education system
- Over 90 per cent of pupils who terminate their full-time educational following completion of the junior-secondary or intermediate stage go into vocational training
- Vocational training is compulsory for anyone not attending another type of school up to the age of 18
- A 'dual system' exists which is a joint initiative between local and central government and private enterprise. The system allows young people to have on-the-job training, as well as instruction in vocational schools

Higher education

- German universities are older than most other European universities and generally their courses last longer. On average, a student will spend 7 years at university completing a degree
- There are around 60 institutions of university status with almost 1.9 million students attending them. In the new federal states (previously East Germany) there are 17 universities

G R E E C E

Working Week	40 hours
Public Holidays	4 compulsory, 2 voluntary (+6 more for banks and government departments)
Paid Holidays	Up to 24
Minimum Wage	Fixed by collective agreements, but may differ according to gender, marital status, length of service, blue/white collar
Sick Pay	26 weeks at 50% with a supplement for dependants
Maternity Leave	16 weeks—14 weeks at 50% of salary paid by state and balance by employer. Single parents can have 6 months' leave
Termination	Blue collar: no statutory notice period White collar: 30 days to 5 months depending on service

Social Protection

- Social protection benefits per capita are one of the lowest in the EU
- There is a system of sick pay for salaried employees, as well as provision for maternity leave
- Old age pensions are financed by insurance schemes; occupational schemes are unusual
- In 1993, Greece spent 15.5 per cent of its GDP on social security provision

Health

- Greece has over 50,000 hospital beds and more than 32,000 doctors for its population
- In 1992, life expectancy was 74.6 for men and 79.8 for women

Education

- The education system is free and starts at the age of 6
- Primary education is compulsory
- In 1987/8 there were over 5,000 kindergartens, more than 8,000 primary schools and almost 3,000 high schools and lycea
- There are 13 universities in Greece

I R E L A N D

Working Week	40 hours
Public Holidays	8
Paid Holidays	3–4 weeks
Minimum Wage	No statutory. About 12% of workers are covered by minimum rates of pay fixed by Joint Labour Committees
Sick Pay	52 weeks paid at a total which must not exceed 75% of weekly earnings
Maternity Leave	4 weeks prior to birth and 4 weeks after, plus an additional 6 weeks paid at 70% of salary
Termination	1–8 weeks depending on service

Social Protection

- Social insurance is compulsory for all employees and the self-employed, and is contributed to by both employers and the state
- There is also a system of social aid with benefits to help people who fall outside the scheme. Typical benefits covered are child benefit, family income supplement and assistance for the elderly
- Social insurance benefits include (amongst others) old age pensions, widows' pensions, disability benefit, invalidity payments, unemployment benefit and maternity benefit
- The Department of Social Welfare also provides a range of benefits in kind mainly for the elderly and disabled. These include free travel, free electricity allowance, free gas allowance, free telephone rental, free TV licence and fuel allowance
- In 1993, Ireland spent 20.4 per cent of its GDP on social security provision

Health

- The Department of Health, under the control of the Minister for Health, is responsible for the Health Service in Ireland, with regional health boards controlling services at local level
- Health care is not entirely free. Lower income groups (around 37 per cent of the population) receive medical services free of charge; for the remainder of the population,

public hospital services and visits to the family doctor are available for a minimal charge. There is a system of voluntary health insurance to help meet the cost of medical treatment
- Ireland is the only country in the EU with a birth rate high enough to be replacing its population; despite this, the birth rate is still falling quite rapidly
- In 1992, life expectancy was 72.6 for men and 78.2 for women.

Education

- In 1990, more than 25 per cent of the country's total population was in full-time education (968,684 people)
- Education is free and compulsory between the ages of 6 and 15

Primary

- Primary education in Ireland is aided by the state but run by local Committees of Management

Secondary

- This level of education covers pupils of age 12 and upwards
- some schools are state-owned, others are state-aided. Many secondary schools are run by religious orders
- Once secondary schooling is completed, pupils may sit the Leaving Certificate examination
- There are 16 comprehensive schools which are financed by the state. These schools combine academic and technical subjects. Pupils take state exams and may go on to enter institutes of further education or universities
- Vocational Education Committee schools provide general and technical education. They are sometimes amalgamated with voluntary secondary schools to form Community schools

Tertiary

- Ireland has four universities, the most famous of which is Trinity College, Dublin University
- There are also regional technical colleges and colleges of technology throughout the country. These institutions focus on applied science and technological education

ITALY

Working Week	40 hours (although 48 hours is the statutory length of the working week)
Public Holidays	9
Paid Holidays	31
Minimum Wage	No statutory minimum wage, but 70% of workers with collective agreements are covered
Sick Pay	All employers are covered by a national plan. Sick pay covered by plan, or employer, or both, funding most or all of salary
Maternity Leave	22 weeks or more. Benefit (taxable) of 80% of gross salary. Optional 6 months with taxable benefit of 30% of gross salary. Parents may work 2 hours less a day for 1 year
Termination	No statutory provision. Covered under collective agreements

Social Protection

- Social protection provision covers pensions, family allowances and health services. Pensions are linked to a price index
- Benefits are paid to families from central government and social security departments
- In 1993, Italy sent 24.5 per cent of its GDP on social security provision

Health

- Italian health services are administered by the *Unità Sanitaria Locale* and are therefore a regional responsibility, although funded by central government
- Medical consultations are free, but since April 1989 patients have had to pay a proportion of prescription costs
- There are approximately 245,000 doctors and 1,300 state hospitals with 350,000 hospital beds
- In 1991, life expectancy was 73.6 for men and 80.3 for women

Education

- There are 2 levels of provision for pre-school education, neither of which is compulsory: day nursery (*nidi d'infanzia*) and nursery school proper (*scuola maternal*)
- Day nurseries are for children under 3 and are often privately run

- Nursery schools are for children aged 3–5 and may be either private ventures or run by religious or local groups
- The general aim of nursery education is to prepare pupils for entry into the compulsory system

Primary

- Primary education is provided by both public and private institutions. The public sector is free and education in both sectors is compulsory between the ages of 6 and 14
- There is a national curriculum system and formal testing takes place at the end of the 5-year period at age 11
- Each pupil has a *scheda* (personal record card) which gives a profile of his or her personality
- The primary school certificate allows progression to secondary education

Secondary

- This may last for 3, 4 or 5 years according to the route taken
- A pupil may complete his/her compulsory education at the *scuola media* (lower secondary school) after 3 years, when a final exam is taken based on a compulsory curriculum. Successful students are awarded a *Diploma di Licenza Media*
- Courses at the higher secondary school (*Liceo*) last 5 years and students are admitted on successful completion of the *scuola media*. The curriculum is compulsory. At the end of a course, successful candidates are awarded a *Diploma di Maturitá*
- Students with a 5-year diploma can proceed to university automatically; holders of the 4-year diploma must first take a special one-year preparatory course
- Higher secondary education is subdivided into classical, scientific and language schools, professional institutes and technical education

Tertiary

- There are 39 state universities in Italy
- Universities are state-run and courses can be of 4, 5 or 6 years' duration
- A degree course is called *Corso di Laurea*. There are also the *Diploma Universitario* and *Laurea Breve*, which are first-line degrees issued after 2 or 3 years of study
- There are also a number of technical institutes in Italy

LUXEMBOURG

Working Week	40 hours
Public Holidays	10 statutory public holidays
Paid Holidays	25 days minimum after 3 months' service
Minimum Wage	Monthly rate for: Unskilled worker — 42,677 Lux/Fr Skilled worker — 51,213 Lux/Fr
Sick Pay	52 weeks at 100% of earnings
Maternity Leave	8 weeks before and 8 weeks after the birth at 100% earnings
Termination	2–6 months depending on service

Social Protection

- Luxembourg has a fairly comprehensive social protection scheme which covers old age pensions, maternity leave and sick pay, among other benefits
- Retirement is normally at 64, although in some circumstances early retirement can be taken either at 57 or 60. Retirement can be deferred until 68
- In 1993, Luxembourg spent 24 per cent of its GDP on social security provision

Health

- The Health Service in Luxembourg provides 9.7 hospital beds per 1,000 habitants (the highest figure in the EU), but only 1.8 doctors per 1,000 inhabitants, which ranks in front of only the UK and Ireland
- In 1992, life expectancy was 71.9 for men and 78.4 for women

Education

- Pre-school education is compulsory for 4-year-olds
- Primary education covers 5–11-year-olds where 3 languages (Letzeburgesch, German and French) are used
- Secondary education covers the ages of 12–15. This can be either general secondary education or technical secondary education
- Higher education focuses on the *Centre Universitaire du Luxembourg*

THE NETHERLANDS

Working Week	40 hours
Public Holidays	8
Paid Holidays	Minimum 15 days, although 23 is the norm and can be as high as 36
Minimum Wage	Payable at 23. Young workers receive a percentage of full rate
Sick Pay	52 weeks at 70% of salary
Maternity Leave	Either parent can work shorter hours for 6 months
Termination	Weekly-paid staff — 1 week Monthly-paid staff — 1 month Additional notice given for employees over 45

Social Protection

- The Dutch enjoy a comprehensive system of social security provision
- Under the Health Insurance Act, anyone with an annual earned income of less than Fl 50,900 (1990) pays a monthly contribution and is then entitled to receive medical, pharmaceutical, dental and hospital treatment. People earning over this amount must take out private medical insurance
- Other benefits available are family allowance, old age pensions, sickness benefit and unemployment benefit. There is also provision made in case of disablement, for widows and orphans and for national assistance
- Workers can access their pensions at the age of 65
- In 1993, the Netherlands spent 32.1 per cent of its GDP on social security provision

Health

- The Netherlands enjoys a high standard of health care. The government's objective, as stated by the Ministry of Foreign Affairs, is 'to create a statutory framework and facilities to prevent disease and accidents and to promote the treatment, nursing and care of those who need it'
- The primary care system operates via GPs and the secondary tier (hospitals) provide specialists
- Health care is financed mainly through an insurance system
- The state does provide some funds, for example, it funds the Municipal Health Services. It is also active in preventive

medicine, funding vaccination programmes for children and school dental services, medical research and the training of health workers
- Most health care facilities are provided by non-governmental and private organisations, many of which began as charities. They are subject to state approval
- In 1991, there were around 38,000 doctors and 65,000 licensed hospital beds
- In 1992, life expectancy was 74.2 for men and 80.3 for women

Education

- Education is compulsory between the ages of 5 and 16
- Compulsory education is generally free, although some schools will ask for a financial contribution from parents
- Freedom of education is guaranteed by the constitution and private and state schools receive equal funding from government
- Approximately 75 per cent of all existing Dutch schools were set up by private bodies and associations
- 4 million of the population are in full-time education

Pre-school

- Play groups and crèches exist, but are not part of the state system and do not come under the control of the Ministry of Education and Science

Primary

- Primary education covers children aged 4–12; school attendance becomes compulsory from the age of 5
- The first 2 years concentrate on the skills of reading, writing, arithmetic and manual skills
- From the age of 6 to 12 the curriculum concentrates on Dutch, maths, writing, history, geography, science and social studies. In the final year at primary schools pupils learn English

Secondary

- There are 3 types of secondary school: general secondary school, pre-university school and vocational secondary school
- Junior and senior schools offer 4 and 5-year courses respectively
- Pre-university schools (called *atheneum* or *gymnasium*) offer 6-year courses in preparation for higher or university education
- Vocational education can be followed at junior, senior or higher level

- Pupils on all of the secondary school courses are required to take written state examinations. The number of subjects taken and the level of the exams vary
- Pupils who leave full-time education at the age of 16 are required by law to attend courses of continued training or education for 1 or 2 days a week

Tertiary

- Higher education includes higher vocational courses at colleges and university education. There are 8 universities and 5 *hogescholen*, which also provide university-level education, and an Open University
- All universities are financed by government funds, irrespective of whether they are state or private foundations
- University courses are split into 2 phases. The first phase takes 4 years and concludes with the *Doctoral* examination. A limited number of students is admitted to the second phase where the student undertakes specialised study or research, leading to a doctorate

P O R T U G A L

Working Week	44 hours maximum
Public Holidays	14 (12 compulsory and 2 optional)
Paid Holidays	22
Minimum Wage	Fixed by government annually. Full rate paid at 20. Some industry sectors fix their own rates in collective agreements
Sick Pay	155 days paid at 65% of the average daily wage. (100% if employee hospitalised and has dependants)
Maternity Leave	98 days (60 to be taken after birth) at 100% of wage
Termination	60 days

Social Protection

- The system of benefits in Portugal is financed partly by employees' and employers' contributions and partly by the state
- There is a general scheme, membership of which is compulsory for the employed and self-employed, and also a non-contributory scheme which protects those who are not covered by the general scheme and who are in need

- The scheme provides protection against unemployment, disability, old age, death, sickness, maternity and work injuries. It also provides family benefits
- Normal retirement age is 65
- In 1993, Portugal spent 17.3 per cent of its GDP on social security provision

Health

- Portugal has the lowest number of hospital beds per 1,000 inhabitants of the EU countries at just 2.9 (the highest is Luxembourg with 9.7)
- In 1989, there were around 28,000 doctors in Portugal
- In 1992, life expectancy was 70.7 for men and 78.1 for women

Education

- Education is compulsory between the ages of 6 and 14
- Pre-school classes cater for 3–6-year-olds. There is free nursery school provision in the public sector
- Primary schools cater for children aged 6–10; from here pupils move into preparatory education, which covers 10–12-year-olds
- Secondary education covers a period of 6 years but is not compulsory beyond age 14. Pupils aged 12–14 follow a general course before they are streamed into specialist areas at the age of 15 or 16. Around the age of 17, the final year of schooling provides 2 routes to the student, either vocational or academic
- There are 14 universities in Portugal, as well as a number of polytechnics

S P A I N

Working Week	40 hours
Public Holidays	14
Paid Holidays	30 working days
Minimum Wage	Payable at 18, the full rate is ESP 62,700 per month (1995). Younger workers receive a percentage
Sick Pay	2–6 months at 60% of earnings for 4–20 days, then 25% thereafter
Maternity Leave	16 weeks (6 must be taken after birth) at 75% of salary
Termination	1–3 months

Social Protection

- The Spanish scheme is funded partly from employees' and employers' contributions, and partly by the state
- The scheme covers retirement pensions, unemployment benefit, disablement allowances, family benefit, health care and sickness benefit, plus some other areas
- The normal retirement age is 65
- In 1993, Spain spent 23.2 per cent of its GDP on social security provision

Health

- The 1978 constitution established the right of every citizen to the protection of health. To this end, the health system has developed fairly quickly over the past 20 years, but not without difficulties
- Current health-care policy aims to reduce social and regional imbalances
- Private hospitals exist alongside the state system, but represent only a small proportion of health care capacity. In 1987, 97.1 per cent of the population was covered by public health care
- In 1991, life expectancy was 73.3 for men and 80.5 for women

Education

- The Spanish education system was overhauled in 1995
- Voluntary, free, pre-school education is available in 2 cycles: 0–3 years and 3–6 years
- Compulsory, free education in schools now covers the ages of 6–16 and comprises 2 stages:
  – primary education (6–12 years)
  – compulsory secondary education (12–16 years)
- Studies can then be pursued via an academic or vocational route
- At 16, students can take the 2-year Baccalaureate course
- Following this a student can continue to university or vocational training

SWEDEN

Working Week	40 hours
Public Holidays	12
Paid Holidays	27 days
Minimum Wage	No legal minimum wage, sometimes fixed by collective bargaining
Sick Pay	Employer pays 2 weeks at 75% of salary for first 3 days, 90% thereafter. State then pays 90% of salary
Maternity Leave	300 days whilst one of the parents may take care of the child. Father is allowed 10 days of paid parental leave on the birth of the child
Termination	1–6 months depending on age

Social Protection

- Sweden has an extensive social protection system covering pensions, social security benefits, unemployment benefits and sickness benefits
- The normal age of retirement is 65, but it is flexible between the ages of 60 and 70

Health

- Primary care is delivered generally via health centres
- Hospitals are provided at county and regional levels via 80 central county hospitals and 10 regional hospitals
- The health system is subsidised, but patients are expected to pay fees subject to a high cost ceiling
- In 1992, life expectancy was 75.4 for men and 80.8 for women

Education

- Education is free and compulsory for a 9-year period
- 4–7: pre-school education
- 7–16: compulsory secondary education
- 16–19: upper secondary
- 19+: university diplomas, general degrees and professional degrees

U K

Working Week	39 hours average, but no legislation on working hours
Public Holidays	8
Paid Holidays	20–27 days
Minimum Wage	No general minimum wage legislation
Sick Pay	28 weeks at between 52–70% of salary
Maternity Leave	18 weeks: 90% pay for 6 weeks, then 12 weeks at standard benefit rate, plus 22 weeks unpaid leave
Termination	Up to 2 years' service – 1 week 2–12 years – 1 week for each complete year

Social Protection

- The National Insurance system funded by government and by employees' and employers' contributions, provides a range of benefits including child benefit, retirement pensions, maternity benefit, statutory sick pay, unemployment benefit, widows' and invalidity benefit
- There is also a form of assistance available for those who have not been able to make adequate contributions
- In 1993, the UK spent 26.7 per cent of its GDP on social security provision

Health

- All people normally resident in the UK are entitled to use the National Health Service (NHS). No insurance qualification is necessary
- The NHS is funded by central government and provides hospitals, general practitioners, dentists and community and school health-care service
- The 190 district health authorities are responsible for the administration and development of health services within each area
- NHS executive has 8 regional offices. The centrally funded health authorities ensure health needs of local communities are met and buy in hospital and community health services

Education

- 4–5: nursery
- 5–11: infant/junior schools (often called primary schools)
- 11–16: secondary education (can be grammar, comprehensive, technical or city technology college)

or in some parts of the country:

- 5–8: first school
- 8–11: middle school
- 11–16: secondary school
- 16–18: secondary school or vocational training at college of further education
- 18+: University or further education

Ethnic Richness within Europe

Whilst the European Union already enjoys the ethnic *mélange* of 15 member states, it is worthwhile remembering the significant numbers of third-country nationals who live within the Union's boundaries. Many of the peoples involved have travelled to the European Union for employment, others have historic ties with the region (ex-colonies) and others sadly may have been driven to seek political asylum.

Great movements of people are evident in the news; for example, the gypsies of Eastern Europe travelling to the UK in 1997, and Albanian boat people landing in Italy in the same year. The following table lists the more significant groupings of citizenship within the member states. It ignores the wider world (the USA) and highlights Greater Europe in general. Where the middle and Far East have been included, it is intended to highlight significant ties with former colonies. The peoples involved have been able to add to and enrich the fabric of European society. The distribution pattern is somewhat skewed and there are one or two countries who sadly miss out on this cultural diversity (Ireland). However, despite some ethnic conflict, fuelled by the recession of the late-1980s and early-1990s, and the short-lived rise of the extreme right-wing parties in some countries, generally third-country nationals are able to live harmoniously in a Europe which is keen to maintain good relations with the outside world.

Population by Citizenship (non-EEA) in EU and EFTA Countries in 1992 (000s)

	Austria	Belgium	Denmark	Germany	Greece	Spain	Finland	France	Ireland	Italy	Luxembourg	Netherlands	Portugal	Sweden	UK
...sh	117	88	32	1,780				198				215		26	29
...er Yugoslavia	198			775				52		21		15		41	15
...a		189		236		63		1,633		170		198	48	23	195
...cco		146		75		50		573		62		164			10
...tan															82
		40		553	39	32		227		86		57			500
															152
...ral & Eastern Europe				550	36			63		21				32	49
...d				271				47						16	29
...ania				92											
...er Soviet Union				51			10								
				98						10				40	
...ia								614							
...ia								206	30						

Source: *Eurostat Yearbook 1995*

Living and Working in Europe ... What Next?

Social protection, health and education schemes sometimes change with the political flavour of each member state. Students may wish to consider:

– Are there any common themes emerging throughout Europe within the educational world, for example, adoption of the baccalaureate as a standard qualification?

– How are member states coping with the increasing costs of social provision?

– How will the costs of social provision affect the development of EMU?

– What effect will the falling birthrate and ageing population have on the economic prosperity of the member states?

3 The EU Treaties and Summits

> **This chapter covers:**
> - ★ How the Community developed
> - ★ The Treaty of Rome: original signatories, objectives, main provisions
> - ★ The Single European Act: background, development, how it amends the Treaty of Rome, implementation
> - ★ The Maastricht Treaty: impetus towards closer union, ratification, scope and importance, subsidiarity, main provisions and amendments to the Treaty of Rome and SEA
> - ★ The role of summits
> - ★ The 1996 Inter-Governmental Conference (IGC)
> - ★ The 1997 Amsterdam Summit

How the EU Developed: A Brief History

The origins of the European Union are to be found in the economic and political history of the period between the First and Second World Wars and in the political and economic structure of Europe after 1945. Between 1918 and 1939, world free trade was increasingly hampered by unilateral actions on the part of countries, the European states and the USA in particular, to gain temporary economic advantage over their main foreign trade rivals. By taking these actions, which included the imposition of tariffs, quotas and competitive devaluations, they hoped to protect their domestic industries and employment. The inter-war period, therefore, saw the principle and practice of free trade slowly disappear as a result of these protectionist interventions, all of which progressively weakened the economies of Europe, assisted in the rise of Nazi Germany, strengthened the forces of nationalism and contributed in part to the Second World War in 1939–45.

Europe after 1945 was very different from the Europe of the early-twentieth-century. No longer was the world dominated by a few powerful European nation states with overseas colonies; now there were two superpowers: the USSR and the USA. No single European state had either the economic or the military resources to enable it to compete with the USA and the USSR on an equal footing.

Drawing on the lessons learnt from the causes of decline of world trade in the inter-war period from 1918–39, and the collapse of many European economies as a direct result of the Second World War, attempts were made to foster international cooperation and recovery through a number of newly formed international organisations. The most important of these were:

- The United Nations (UN)
- The International Monetary Fund (IMF)
- The International Bank for Reconstruction and Development (World Bank)
- The General Agreement on Tariffs and Trade (GATT) – now the World Trade Organisation

All of these, however, were global arrangements with a strong US influence. The nations of Western Europe, none of which retained the economic, political or military status that they had enjoyed prior to 1939, felt the need for some form of collective arrangement for the mutual protection of their frontiers and for the development of policies to prevent recurrence of the economic rivalries that had existed before 1939. The period up to 1950 consequently saw the establishment of several organisations which, though they had different specific concerns, all shared the aim of encouraging cooperation among Western European states.

BRUSSELS TREATY ORGANISATION, 1948

The Brussels Treaty was signed in 1948 and related to defence matters. It immediately preceded the North Atlantic Treaty which was signed in 1949. The Brussels Treaty was signed at the beginning of the Cold War at a time when the signatories, Belgium France, Luxembourg, the Netherlands and the UK, were concerned about a revival of German militarism.

THE COUNCIL OF EUROPE, 1949

The Council of Europe (not to be confused with the European Council, part of the organisational structure of the European Community – see Chapter 4) was established in 1949 as a means of increasing diplomatic cooperation between its signatories. The competence of the Council was, and is, very wide, but the UK and some other signatories resisted any moves to give the Council supranational rather than intergovernmental powers.

ORGANISATION FOR EUROPEAN ECONOMIC COOPERATION (OEEC), 1948

The OEEC grew out of the immediate post-war need to distribute aid made available to Europe from the USA as part of the Marshall plan. It was an intergovernmental organisation established initially in 1948, and it laid the foundation for the creation of the much wider Organisation for Economic Cooperation and Development (OECD), which was set up in 1961.

It was still felt, however, that although the formation of these groupings was a positive step, they could not achieve the objectives of economic growth and the protection of frontiers. It became clear that only by a stronger economic union could real progress be made. Accordingly, during the period 1951–57, negotiations took place which led to the establishment of the European Economic Community, the European Coal and Steel Community, the European Atomic Energy Community and the European Defence Community.

The decision to proceed in this direction was not, however, a unanimous one; the UK in particular was conspicuous by not being a party to it. British reticence was due in part to the fact that the UK still had a large market for its goods in the remains of its Empire and was not, therefore, ready to adopt a primarily European perspective on trade. Also, there was a growing belief on mainland Europe that a genuinely workable economic union could not be achieved without a degree of political union and that this would inevitably mean a loss or pooling of sovereignty in certain key areas. Britain was not willing to accept this. The debate concerning federation or a United States of Europe first appeared in a serious form during this period and was to resurface in the 1980s.

The Treaty of Rome (1957)

The Original Members of the EEC

The Treaty of Rome, which created the European Economic Community and the European Atomic Energy Community, was signed by six countries on 27 March 1959. Membership was not, however, strictly limited to the founding six member states; 'associate status' membership was created to cater for those countries which had previously enjoyed strong political and economic links with full member states. Countries accorded associate status were able to trade with, and obtain aid from the EEC on preferential terms.

ORIGINAL SIGNATORIES TO THE TREATY OF ROME

Belgium
France
Italy
Luxembourg
Netherlands
West Germany

Total population: 180 million

ASSOCIATE MEMBERS OF THE EEC

Greece (now a full member)
Israel
Malta
Morocco
Tunisia
Turkey
Spain (now a full member)

Total population: 70 million

The Objectives of the Treaty

The Treaty not only set out the policies of the EEC, but also crated the institutions which would develop and implement these policies. Article 2 of the Treaty of Rome states:

> The Community shall have as its task by establishing a common market and progressively approximating the economic policies of member states, to promote throughout the Community a harmonious development of economic activities, a continuous and balanced expansion, an increase instability, an accelerated raising of the standard of living and closer relations between the states belonging to it.

This article clearly reflects the anxieties of the signatories which gave rise to their desire for closer economic and political cooperation.

Article 3 sets out the activities by which the Community would try to achieve the objectives identified in Article 2. The text carefully says that the activities set out shall 'include' the steps mentioned, thus implying that other steps not mentioned in the

Treaty may later be taken to promote the development of the Community.

Free-Trade Area or Customs Union?

The original purpose of the Treaty of Rome was to promote the prosperity and economic expansion of its members by the creation of a customs union. This meant that all the countries of the Community agreed that in relation to trade with outside countries they would operate a common external tariff.

Once goods enter a country in a customs union from a country outside the union, they move freely within the customs area without attracting further duty when crossing an internal border. In a free-trade area, on the other hand, this concession applies only to goods which are manufactured in that area.

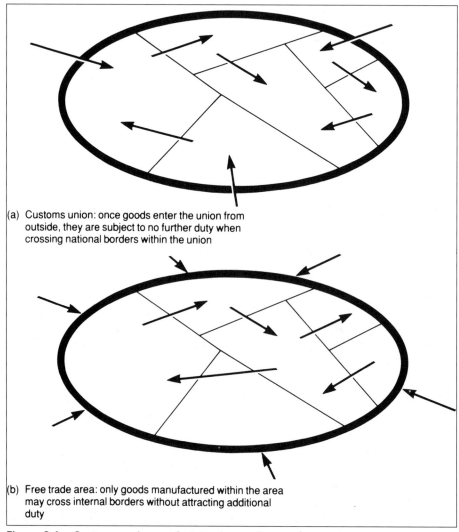

(a) Customs union: once goods enter the union from outside, they are subject to no further duty when crossing national borders within the union

(b) Free trade area: only goods manufactured within the area may cross internal borders without attracting additional duty

Figure 3.1   Customs union or free-trade area?

A customs union is therefore surrounded by a 'ring fence' which protects the internally-produced goods, but ensures that all goods, whether manufactured internally or not, move freely once within the fenced area. Such a policy obviously protects industry and business within the common market it creates.

Article 3 of the Treaty of Rome does in fact provide for the elimination of customs duties between member states, but this and several other provisions of the Treaty were not fully adopted or enforced for many years after signature. The impetus for the elimination of customs duties came from the Single European Act and was only finally ensured after 1 January 1993. It is important to understand that the EC did not originally create a free-trade area within its borders.

The New European Institutions

The institutions of the European Economic Community which were created by Article 4 of the Treaty of Rome were a European Parliament, a Council, a Commission and a Court of Justice. The Treaty set out the powers of these institutions and also created an Economic and Social Committee to advise the Council and the Commission, and a Court of Auditors to monitor the Community's financial affairs.

The Single European Act (1986)

The Need for a New Treaty

By the early 1980s, the structure of European industry still reflected an uncommon and divided market. For example, different standards applying in different countries forced many countries to manufacture separate products for each national market, thereby preventing them benefiting from economies of scale and so lowering their costs and becoming more profitable. The common market had become, by the early 1980s, the 'uncommon market'. The EC was failing to make effective use of its collective resources and was creating unnecessary costs for businesses.

The Community realised that without a stronger economic framework, fundamental weaknesses would prevent the EC from achieving the goals of its founders set out in the Treaty of Rome. Moreover, in the increasingly competitive, international economic environment, the EC would remain at a disadvantage in relation to its major competitors, Japan and the USA. As a result of this failure to progress, individual citizens of the member states would be unable to enjoy the economic advantages that should have been theirs.

THE TREATY OF ROME AS AMENDED BY THE SINGLE EUROPEAN ACT

Part 1	*Establishes the principles of the European Economic Community*
Article 1	Creates the European Economic Community
Article 2	Outlines the task of the Community
Article 3	Sets out a list of activities which the Community shall undertake
Article 4	Creates the institutions
Article 5	Exhorts member states to facilitate and not jeopardise the Treaty objectives
Article 6	States that member states shall coordinate their respective economic policies
Article 7	Enshrines the principle of non-discrimination on the grounds of nationality
Article 8	Gives transitional provisions
Part 2	*Sets out the foundation of the Community*
Articles 9–37	Free movement of goods
Articles 38–47	Agriculture
Articles 48–58	Free movement of workers and the right of establishment
Articles 59–66	Freedom to provide services
Articles 67–73	Free movement of capital
Articles 74–84	Transport
Part 3	*Sets out the policies of the Community*
Articles 85–90	Competition policy
Article 91	Dumping
Article 92	Aids granted by states
Articles 95–98	Tax provisions
Articles 99–102	Approximation of laws
Article 102a–109	Economic policy, conjunctural payments and balance of payments
Articles 110–116	Commercial policy
Articles 117–128	Social policy and the European Social Fund
Articles 129–130	The European Investment Bank
Articles 130a–130e	Economic and social cohesion
Articles 130f–130g	Research and technological development
Articles 130–130t	Environment
Part 4	
Articles 131–136a	Set out the relationship of the Community with associate countries and territories

Part 5	Creates the institutions of the Community
Articles 137–144	The European Parliament
Articles 145–153	The Council:
Article 154	Repealed by the SEA
Article 155	The Commission:
Articles 156–163	Repealed by the SEA
Articles 164–188	The Court of Justice
Articles 189–192	Common provisions
Articles 193–298	The Economic and Social Committee
Article 199–209	Financial provisions
Part 6	
Articles 210–247	General and financial provisions

The Development of the SEA

At the beginning of 1985, the newly appointed President of the Commission, Jacques Delors, suggested to the leaders of the member states that steps should be taken to revitalise the Community by removing all non-tariff barriers to trade and attempting to complete the internal market. A summit of EC leaders held in Milan in June 1985, set up an Inter-Governmental Conference to look at the possibility of achieving the Single European Market by 1992. The basis for discussion was the document published by the Commission in May 1985, entitled *Completing the Internal Market*, which set out a detailed legislative programme and timetable.

The Luxembourg Summit in December 1985, resulted in a clear acceptance by all member states that the internal market should be completed by the end of 1992 and that the legal measures necessary should stem from an amendment to the Treaty of Rome. This became known as the Single European Act. This Act was ratified by all member states during 1987.

The Content of the SEA

THE AIMS OF THE SINGLE EUROPEAN ACT, AS SET OUT IN THE PREAMBLE

1 To continue the work undertaken already and transform relations among member states into a European union.
2 To implement a common foreign policy.
3 To promote democracy and fundamental rights and freedoms – notably freedom, equality and social justice.
4 To aim at speaking ever-increasingly with one voice and to act with consistency and solidarity.
5 To improve the economic and social situation by extending common policies and pursuing new objectives.

The central intention of the Act's architects was that the SEA should provide the necessary political impetus and legal framework to achieve a unified market by 1 January 1993. The Act defined the single market as 'an area without internal frontiers in which the free movement of goods, persons, services and capital is ensured'.

The SEA is a wide-ranging document, covering much more than the single market. It sets out a number of amendments to the original founding treaties and covers subjects such as economic and social cohesion, the environment, cooperation between the various European institutions and greater political cooperation. It also underlines the commitment of the European Community to achieving the aims of the original treaties.

In the specific, and sometimes controversial, terms for which he became well known, Jacques Delors (then President of the European Commission), stated the following objectives for the Single European Market:

- The creation of a single market without frontiers
- To ensure cooperation on monetary policy
- To highlight social policy
- To ensure progress on 'green' issues
- To enhance cooperation in the areas of technology and research and development
- To further develop and introduce regional structural policies

The SEA in Action

Between the passing of the Single European Act in 1986, and the 1 January 1993 completion date for the SEM, over 80 per cent of more than 300 measures necessary for the creation of the single market had been passed and put into effect. By 1998, however, many steps remained to be taken before the single market was truly complete. Political problems have led to deadlock in some key areas, and national administrative systems have not always caught up with policy decisions taken at European level (see section on the IGC on page 115).

Summits

The European Union operates on the basis of a six-monthly rotation of the Presidency of the Council of Ministers (see Chapter 4). This Presidency is held by a country and at the end of the Presidency a conference (summit) takes place in that country. Presidencies, and subsequent summits, are opportunities for the country holding the Presidency to promote those policies it wishes to see adopted. The Maastricht Summit, at which the Maastricht Treaty was adopted, is perhaps the best known.

The Maastricht Treaty

Background: Towards a Closer Union

The logical extension of many of the principles contained in the Single European Act is an ever-closer union, with the influence of the Community reaching more and more deeply into the affairs of the member states. By the late 1980s, the pull in this direction had come to be felt particularly strongly on two fronts, towards:

- economic and monetary union and
- political union, including a common foreign and security policy

Not all the member states were equally enthusiastic about this trend. Britain, under the premiership of Mrs Thatcher, was notable for its reservations, favouring a looser, wider grouping incorporating a larger number of member states. However, others – the so-called 'federalists', who included the President of the Commission, Jacques Delors – believed that the time had come to consolidate and deepen the ties among the existing members, to develop more common policies and more powerful Community institutions to promote and enforce them.

THE MAASTRICHT TREATY, 1: OBJECTIVES

Article A
The creation of a European union of states founded on the European communities and added to by the provisions of this treaty.

Article B

- The creation of an area without internal frontiers
- The strengthening of economic and social cohesion
- The establishment of economic and monetary union
- Ultimately, the creation of a single currency
- The implementation of a common foreign and security policy
- The introduction of citizenship of the European Union
- The development of close cooperation in justice and home affairs

Article C
The institutions of the European Community shall continue to serve the European Union and ensure the consistency of its policies.

Article D
The European Council which comprises the heads of government shall instigate measures to promote the European Union and define its political direction.

> **Article E**
> Confirms that the institutions of the European Community shall continue to exercise their responsibilities as before and shall receive additional and modified responsibilities under this treaty.
>
> **Article F**
> Confirms the respect which the signatories have for the national identity of member states and human rights within them as agreed by the European Convention on Human Rights.

During 1989 and 1990, it was decided that two intergovernmental conferences should be convened: one on economic and monetary union and one on political union, to consider a new Community Treaty. The ensuring debate began in Rome in December 1990 and concluded in Maastricht in December 1991.

The Problem of Ratification

On 11 December 1991, the European Community leaders agreed the text of a treaty on European Union and Economic Monetary Union – known as the Maastricht Treaty from the place where agreement was reached. The member states agreed that in order to take effect, the Treaty would have to be ratified by each individual country according to its own constitutional procedures.

The constitutions of Denmark, France and Ireland require that a referendum is held to confirm or reject the government's decision to adopt any measure with constitutional significance for the country. The Maastricht Treaty, with far-reaching implications for the national independence of the EC member states, was therefore subject to a referendum in each of these three countries.

While the voters in France and Ireland approved the Treaty, albeit by fairly narrow majorities, those of Denmark rejected it in the referendum held on 2 June 1992. The Danish government conducted a campaign designed to change the voters' minds, and a second referendum on 18 May 1993 resulted in a 'yes' vote.

In Britain, where opinion on the future of the Community was sharply divided, calls for a referendum on ratification of the Treaty were firmly rejected by the government of John Major, which maintained that under the British constitution it was for the government to take responsibility for all its treaty contracts.

The Treaty came into force throughout all member states in 1993 after the last signatory state had ratified it.

Maastricht: Its Scope and Importance

When asked why the Maastricht Treaty was so important, the

Commission President, Jacques Delors, identified five main reasons (*The European*, 17 September 1992):

- It would give Europe the strength essential for success in world markets
- It would foster peaceable relations in a working society that was increasingly fragmented
- The Community must move forward, escaping the stagnation that has beset it in the past
- Through this Treaty, member states will be more closely involved in Community affairs
- Without the Maastricht Treaty the future of the Community, and of Europe as a whole, is uncertain and dangerous

The crucial point about the Maastricht Treaty is that it extends the scope of the Community into areas that have hitherto been exclusively the province of national governments. Some of these areas are incorporated into the institutional framework established by the Treaty of Rome; some, such as the common foreign and security policy, remain outside the formal institutional base of the EC.

Other important general points about the Treaty are:

- It creates a common policy on judicial affairs
- It gives added emphasis to the European Council of Heads of Government as the major force for future policy making
- It gives the European Parliament increased powers of decision making and inquiry, and increased rights to be consulted

---

THE MAASTRICHT TREATY, 2: AMENDMENTS TO THE TREATY OF ROME

The term 'European Economic Community' shall be replaced by 'European Community'.

Article 2
Article 2 of the Treaty of Rome shall be replaced by a new wider Article 2 which encompasses the promotion of a harmonious and balanced development of economic activities, sustainable and non-inflationary growth, respecting the environment, a high degree of convergence of economic performance, a high level of employment and social protection, the raising of the standard of living and quality of life, and economic and social cohesion and solidarity among member states.

Article 3
A new Article 3, replacing the previous Article 3 of the Treaty of Rome, provides that the activities of the Community shall include the provisions set out below, which shall be implemented within the agreed timetable.

Article 3A

This is an addition to the Treaty of Rome and provides:

For the adoption by the Community of an economic policy based on the close coordination of member states' economic policies on the internal market and the definition of common objectives. This shall include the irrevocable fixing of exchange rates, the introduction of a single currency and a single monetary and exchange rate policy.

Member states shall comply with certain guiding principles as to stable prices, sound public finances and monetary conditions, and a sustainable balance of payments:

(a) The elimination, as between member states, of customs duties and quantitative restrictions on the import and export of goods and of all other measures having equivalent effect.

(b) A common commercial policy.

(c) An internal market characterised by the abolition, as between member states, of obstacles to the free movements of goods, persons, services and capital.

(d) Measures concerning the entry and movement of persons in the internal market as provided for in Article 100C.

(e) A common policy in the sphere of transport.

(f) A system ensuring that competition in the internal market is not distorted.

(g) The approximation of the laws of member states to the extent required for the functioning of the common market.

(h) A policy in the social sphere comprising a European Social Fund.

(i) The strengthening of economic and social cohesion.

(j) A policy in the sphere of the environment.

(k) The strengthening of competitiveness of Community industry.

(l) The promotion of research and technological development.

(m) Encouragement for the establishment and development of trans-European networks.

(n) A contribution to the attainment of a high level of health protection.

(o) A contribution to education and training of quality and to the flowering of the cultures of the member states.

(p) A policy in the sphere of development cooperation.

(q) The association of the overseas countries and territories in order to increase trade and promote joint economic and social development.

(r) A contribution to the strengthening of consumer protection.

(s) Measures in the spheres of energy, civil protection and tourism.

Article 3B (Subsidiarity)

A new Article which seeks to establish that the European Community should not pass legal rules where the same results can be achieved by member states themselves passing legislation. In other words, the principle of subsidiarity is now part of the constitution of the Community and the Community shall not pass any rules which go beyond what is necessary to achieve the objectives of the Treaty.

> **Article 4**
> Confirms the institution of the European Community and creates, as well as the Economic and Social Committee, a committee of the regions to act in an advisory capacity.
>
> **Article 4A**
> Provides for the establishment of the European system of central banks and the European central banks.

Subsidiarity

The text of the Treaty reflects the compromise reached after lengthy and difficulty debate between the 'federalists' and those who resisted any further encroachment of European powers on national affairs – whom one might call the 'nationalists'. A key concept in reaching this compromise was that of 'subsidiarity', by which is meant that decisions should be taken as close to the point of impact as possible, and that any action by the Community shall not go beyond what is necessary to achieve the objectives of the Treaty (see Article 3B).

The compromise between 'federalists' and 'nationalists' is encapsulated in a phrase from the preamble to the Treaty itself:

This Treaty marked a new stage in the process of creating an ever-closer union among the people of Europe, where decisions are taken as closely as possible to the citizens.

Details of Britain's opt-out from the Social Chapter of the Treaty will be found in Chapter 8.

The 1996 Inter-Governmental Conference (IGC)

It was stated earlier that the Single European Market still had areas which prevented it from being regarded as complete. In 1995, a European Commission report highlighted a number of areas where further progress was required:

- Completion of the SEM for the citizen
- Promotion of the SEM for business
- Ensuring harmonisation of enforcement of EU legislation in all member countries
- Encouraging the countries of eastern and central Europe (some of whom are candidates for early entry to the EU) to meet SEM requirements
- Liberalising energy supply

- Liberalising telecommunications
- Preparing for the 'information society'

In the spring of 1996, the Inter-Governmental Conference to revise the Maastricht Treaty and evaluate the effectiveness of the SEM was instituted. This Conference (not a single event but extending over both the Dublin and Amsterdam Summits, in addition to other meetings) ended at Amsterdam and its achievements are best summed up by examining the events at the Summit.

The Amsterdam Summit

The run-up to the June 1997 Amsterdam Summit was not particularly optimistic. The Dublin Summit of 1996 had been dominated by disagreement between France and Germany over a 'stability pact' restricting borrowing by countries joining the single currency. Fears were that this issue would overshadow a very important summit intended to bring together the work of the IGC and to adopt a new treaty to revise that of Maastricht.

The new Treaty may be regarded, in the words of Lionel Jospin, the French Prime Minster, as a 'reasonable step'. Key elements are:

- Formal negotiations opening the European Union to central and eastern European members were scheduled to begin by the end of 1997
- Treaty provision on asylum, immigration and visas
- The Schengen zone (see page 151), over a period, to come under the administrative influence of the Commission, Parliament and Court. However, most issues of justice and home affairs will remain subject to unanimous vote by the Council of Ministers
- The UK and Ireland are guaranteed an indefinite control over their own borders
- Research will be governed by majority voting of the Council of Ministers
- Foreign policy which is agreed may be implemented by majority vote, but with the proviso that if a country's 'special national interest' is threatened, they may exercise a veto
- The ability of countries to adopt policies that not all are adopting and to do this under majority voting. Again with the 'special national interest' veto

Areas of dissent involved:

- France's desire to balance the 'stability pact' on borrowing with measures to create jobs and protect employment – vague acknowledgments are made to France's position
- Germany and France's desire for the EU to absorb the

Western European Union and so obtain its own defence capability – not happening at present

- The issues of voting weights in the Council of Ministers (larger countries have more effective votes) and the Commission's size. No agreement was reached on reform of these and change was deferred – essentially the smaller countries are resisting any changes which will reduce their say. In practical terms, the lack of reform could hinder the expansion of the Union

The EC Treaties and Summits ... What Next?

Students should examine the areas identified as requiring action prior to the 1996 IGC in the context of the Amsterdam Treaty provisions, and evaluate progress made in the period up to, and beyond, the Millennium.

4 The Institutions of the Community

This chapter describes:

The institutions created by the Treaty of Rome, including:

★ The Commission
★ The European Council
★ The Council of Ministers
★ The Parliament
★ The Court of Justice
★ The Economic and Social Committee
★ The European Investment Bank

The institutions created by the Single European Act (European Court of First Instance) and the Maastricht Treaty (Committee of Permanent Representatives).

The European Commission

Composition

The 20 Commissioners are nominated by the governments of the member states. The larger states nominate two Commissioners each, other states nominate one each, as follows:

• France, Germany, Italy, Spain and the UK: two Commissioners each
• Belgium, Denmark, Greece, Ireland, Luxembourg, the Netherlands, Finland, Sweden, Austria, Portugal: one Commissioner each

The members of the Commission are technically appointed by the European Council. Attempts in the past by the President of the Commission to influence the nominations have been strongly resisted. Any alteration in the total number of Commissioners can be decided only by unanimous decision of the European Council

Each Commissioner holds office for five years, after which he or she may be replaced by another appointee or reappointed for a further five years. The President and Vice Presidents of the Commission are elected by the Commissioners from the body of the Commission. The Commissioners pledge allegiance to the EU.

Functions

The functions and powers of the Commission, as set out in Article 155 of the Treaty of Rome, are:

- To ensure that the provisions of the Treaty are applied
- To formulate recommendations or deliver opinions
- To decide and participate in the shaping of measures taken by the Council and the European Parliament
- To exercise the powers conferred on it by the Council

The Commission is responsible for the implementation of Union policy. It may also initiate Union policy by putting items on the agenda for discussion by the Council of Ministers. Each Commissioner is responsible for a particular area of Union policy. Each policy area has a Director-General and staff to carry out and oversee the implementation of policy.

THE COMMISSIONER'S OATH

I solemnly undertake:

- To perform my duties in complete independence, in the general interests of the Community
- In carrying out my duties, neither to seek nor to take instructions from any government or body
- To refrain from any action incompatible with my duties
- I formally note the undertaking of each member state to respect this principle and not to seek to influence members of the Commission in the performance of their task
- I further undertake to respect, both during and after my term of office, the obligations arising therefrom, and in particular the duty to behave with integrity and discretion as regards the acceptance, after I have ceased to hold office, of certain appointments or benefits

---

THE EUROPEAN COMMISSION (JUNE 1997)

Name	Country	Position
Jacques Santer	Luxembourg	President
Carlo Trojan	Netherlands	Secretary-General
Franz Fischler	Austria	Agriculture
Erkki Liikanen	Finland	Budget
Karel Van Miert	Belgium	Competition
Yves-Thibault de Silguy	France	Economic and Financial Affairs
Christos Papoutis	Greece	Energy

Ritt Bjerregaard	Denmark	Environment
Sir Leon Brittan	UK	External Relations
Hans van den Broek	Netherlands	External Relations
Manuel Marin	Spain	External Relations
João de Deus Pinheiro	Portugal	External Relations
Emma Bonino	Italy	Fisheries, Consumer Policy
Anita Gradin	Sweden	Immigration, Interior & Judicial Affairs
Martin Bangemann	Germany	Industrial Policy
Marcelino Oreja	Spain	Institutional Questions
Mario Monti	Italy	Internal Market
Monika Wulf-Mathies	Germany	Regional Policy
Edith Cresson	France	Science, Research and Development
Padraig Flynn	Ireland	Social Affairs and Employment
Neil Kinnock	UK	Transport

In essence, the Commission is there to protect the interests of the Union, and accordingly Commissioners are required to act in the interests of the Commission, and not in the interests of individual countries or the governments which appoint them. In the course of promoting and protecting Union interests, the Commission may bring an action against a member state if it considers that there has been a breach of an obligation of the Treaty. Article 169 of the Treaty of Rome states:

> If the Commission considers that a member state has failed to fulfil an obligation under this Treaty, it shall deliver a reasoned opinion on the matter after giving the state concerned the opportunity to submit its observations. If the state concerned does not comply with the opinion within the period laid down by the Commission, the latter may bring the matter before the Court of Justice.

DIRECTORATES-GENERAL OF THE EUROPEAN COMMUNITY

1	External economic relations
1a	External political relations
2	Economic and financial affairs
3	Internal market and industrial affairs
4	Competition
5	Employment, social affairs and education
6	Agriculture
7	Transport
8	Development
9	Personnel and administration
10	Information, communication and culture
11	Environment, consumer protection and nuclear safety

12	Science, research and development
13	Telecommunications, information industry and innovation
14	Fisheries
15	Internal market and financial services
16	Regional policy
17	Energy
18	Credit and investments
19	Budget
20	Financial control
21	Customs union and indirect taxation
22	Education, training and youth
23	Small and medium-sized enterprises
24	Consumer policy

Figure 4.1   The Berlaymont building where the European Commission is located.

Source: European Commission

Part of the reason for the provision of this power is to ensure that the custody of the policies and practices of the Union are in the hands of a neutral body, and that the guardianship of the Treaties is not left to individual member states.

In practice, some 75 per cent of cases brought under Article 169 are settled by agreement between member states and the Commission and no hearing before the European Court of Justice is necessary. Following the ratification of the Maastricht Treaty, increased powers given to the Court of Justice will permit it to fine member states for non-compliance with its rulings.

The UK has been the subject of many complaints to the Commission, some of which have resulted in actions under Article 169. The most common areas of complaint are:

- equal opportunities for men and women
- environmental matters
- fisheries matters

One of the most famous cases involving the UK under Article 169 was *Commission* v. *UK re Merchant Shipping Rules* (Case 246/89R). This case was part of the group of cases which arose out of the British government's introduction of rules which prohibited non-UK registered vessels from fishing in British waters. The new rules prohibited foreign owners to register their boats as British and thereby bypass the prohibition (see Chapter 5). The European Court of Justice ordered the suspension of the Merchant Shipping Act pending the full hearing, thus confirming the supremacy of the Community over domestic law and leading to the headline in *The European* on 26 July 1991, 'Spanish Fishermen 1; British Sovereignty 0'.

The European Council

Composition

The European Council consists of the heads of government of the member states. This group usually meets twice a year; these meetings are often called the 'European Summits'.

Functions

The European Council deliberates on matters of high strategy with respect to the development of the Union, particularly steps towards closer integration. Issues for discussion may be put on the Council's agenda by members of the European Council itself, or by the Commission.

The Council's decisions or recommendations may be either sent on to the Commission for implementation, or referred to the Parliament.

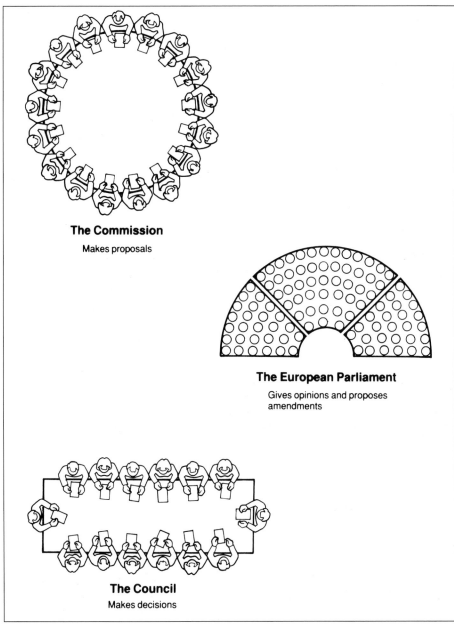

The Commission

Makes proposals

The European Parliament

Gives opinions and proposes
amendments

The Council

Makes decisions

Figure 4.2   The three central institutions of the Union

The Council of Ministers

The Council of Ministers is an entirely different body from the
European Council. Its membership varies, as it consists of the
Minister from each member state with national responsibility for
whichever area of activity is under discussion. Thus, for example,
the Council of Ministers may consist at one time of the Agriculture

Ministers of all the member states, and at another, of all the Ministers for Home Affairs, Ministers of the Interior, the British Home Secretary, etc.

The Council of Ministers is envisaged by the Union Treaties as the body responsible for the formulation of Union policy. Using the same example, the Council of Agriculture Ministers would deliberate on, and draw up, agricultural policy, and the Council of Home Affairs Ministers would address questions of immigration or crime policy.

The Committee of Permanent Representatives (COREPER)

The Maastricht Treaty created a new Article 155 in the Treaty of Rome by which the Committee of Permanent Representatives was brought into being. This body is responsible for preparing the work of the Council of Ministers and carrying out tasks assigned to it by the Council of Ministers.

Qualified majority voting

The Single European Act of 1986 introduced the principle of qualified majority voting, or QMV. The introduction of this system has enabled the Union to make progress on issues which before 1986 would have been totally blocked by the dissension of one or two member states.

Many articles of the Treaty of Rome originally required decisions of the Council of Ministers to be unanimous, and some still do. Such articles include:

* the admission of a new member
* the location of the institutions of the Union
* fiscal measures

The Single European Act extended the provision of QMV to cover matters necessary for the completion of the single market. Other non-single market issues remained subject to the 'right of veto' which was established by virtue of the 'Luxembourg Compromise' in 1966. This informal agreement between member states gives an individual right of veto to a member state where 'very important interests' of that member state were at stake.

The Commission was criticised in the run-up to 1992 for including in the single market programme, measures which might not naturally have found themselves there, in order to take advantage of the QMV provision.

QUALIFIED MAJORITY VOTING (QMV)

This is a system of weighted voting whereby the Council of Ministers can, in certain circumstances, make decisions even if not all states are in agreement. Each state is allocated a number of votes as follows:

Country	No. of Votes
Austria	4
Belgium	5
Denmark	3
Finland	3
France	10
Germany	10
Greece	5
Ireland	3
Italy	10
Luxembourg	2
Netherlands	5
Portugal	5
Spain	8
Sweden	4
UK	10
Total	**87 votes**

The weightings were drawn up to reflect the relative populations of member states. A majority is at least 62 votes cast by at least 10 members. 26 votes are necessary to block a proposal, 23 votes will give a temporary blocking minority.

The European Parliament

Composition

The Parliament, which is based in Strasbourg, consists of 626 members directly elected by the voters of each member state. The number of seats allocated to each country is shown in the following box.

Elections have taken place every five years since 1979; the last elections were held in 1994 and the next are due to be held in 1999. The first direct elections to the Parliament took place in 1979; before this date the Assembly (as it was known before the Single European Act) consisted of 142 delegates *chosen* from the national parliaments of member states.

Once elected to the Parliament, members (MEPs) align themselves with their party groupings, not according to the countries they represent. Thus, for example, British Labour MEPs, French Socialist members and German Social Democrats would all consider themselves part of the Socialist grouping. Obviously because the precise orientations of analogous parties differ from country to country, these groupings are less homogenous than any national political party.

A President and 14 Vice-Presidents are elected by the members for a two and a half-year term. The President takes the chair at the plenary sessions of the Parliament (12 minimum are held throughout the year in Strasbourg and Brussels) and, together with the Vice-Presidents (who are generally referred to as The Bureau), s/he is responsible for the organisation of the work of the Parliament. The Bureau determines how work is to be conducted and decides on the membership and organisation of the 18 standing committees of the Parliament where much of the detailed work is carried out. Broadly, these committees correspond to the Directorates-General of the Commission.

The Parliament is supported by a secretariat.

Functions and Powers

It is important to understand that the European Parliament does not have the law-making function of a national parliament. The Treaty of Rome speaks in terms of 'advisory and supervisory powers'. However, over the years the Parliament has gained additional power by virtue of decisions of the European Court of Justice and amendments to the original Treaty provisions. It has general powers of supervision in relation to the Commission and consults with the Council. It votes to approve the appointed

---

THE EUROPEAN PARLIAMENT, I: COMPOSITION

Country	No. of Seats
Austria	21
Belgium	25
Denmark	16
France	87
Germany	99
Greece	25
Ireland	15
Italy	87
Luxembourg	6
Netherlands	31
Portugal	25
Spain	64
UK	87
Total seats	**626**

Figure 4.3   The European Parliament

Source: European Commission

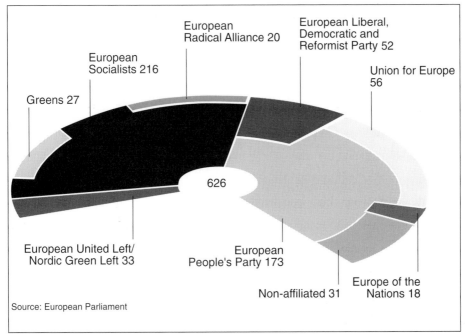

Figure 4.4   The European Parliament: Distribution of seats by political group as at 1 October 1996

Source: *Key Figures*, Eurostat

Commission and has the right to dismiss it. It can also reject the EU budget.

The Single European Act enhanced the consultative role of the Parliament; also Article 6 provides that the Council of Ministers and the Parliament shall cooperate on the introduction of measures to implement the single market.

The Maastricht Treaty gives significant additional power to the Parliament under Article 138.

- It gives the Parliament, for the first time, the power of veto over proposals for legislation in some areas
- It creates an arbitration procedure for occasions when the Council of Ministers and the Parliament cannot agree on legislative proposals

It is evident that the European Parliament has gradually expanded its influence due to the Single European Act and the Maastricht Treaty.

The European Court of Justice

Composition

The Court consists of 15 judges appointed by the governments of the member states. The Treaty of Rome does not provide that each member state shall have a judge in the Court, but this has become customary.

In practice, only on the most important cases will all judges be present. For routine cases and for the purpose of making preliminary recommendations, the judges divide into groups of three or six known as 'chambers'.

The Advocates General, of whom there are nine, are equal in status to the judges. Their main function is to assist the judges by giving an opinion prior to that of the court itself. Advocates General give opinions individually and, in general, the court will not always follow their recommendations.

Functions

The functions and powers of the European Court of Justice are set out in Articles 169–81 of the Treaty of Rome. The Court has jurisdiction (*inter alia*):

- to hear cases between member states where there has been a failure to fulfil the requirements of the Treaty
- to hear action brought by the Commission against member states for breaches of the Treaty
- to hear action brought by member states against the

institutions of the Union for infringement or misuse of their powers

- under Article 177, to give preliminary rulings on the interpretation of the Treaty

In addition, the Maastricht Treaty gives the Court the power to fine member states who do not implement legislation within designated time scales.

The European Court of First Instance

Composition

The Court consists of 15 members, one from each member state, who elect a President from among their number, who serves for a renewable term of three years. This court does not have Advocates General.

Functions

The purpose of the Court of First instance, which was established by the Single European Act, is primarily to reduce the workload of the European Court of Justice.

The Court has jurisdiction (*inter alia*):

- to hear disputes between the Union and its employees

- to hear action against the institutions of the Union brought by member states or other persons or institutions, on the grounds of misuse of power, lack of competence or breach of procedure

The Court of Auditors

The Court of Auditors was instituted in 1975 by the Budgetary Powers Treaty. Fifteen members are nominated, one by each member state, for a six-year term which may be renewed.

The Court of Auditors, as its name implies, has the task of auditing the accounts of the various institutions and bodies of the Community. Unlike business auditors, its remit is not simply to check that expenditure has been properly incurred and can be accounted for, but, like the UK Audit Commission, that unnecessary waste has not occurred.

It was this latter point that led the Court to cricitise the other institutions of the Union for the huge costs of maintaining diverse locations for Union institutions.

The Economic and Social Committee

There are 222 members of the Economic and Social Committee allocated as set out in the following box.

THE ECONOMIC AND SOCIAL COMMITTEE

Country	No. of Members	Country	No. of Members
Austria	12	Italy	24
Belgium	12	Luxembourg	6
Denmark	9	Netherlands	12
Finland	9	Portugal	12
France	24	Spain	21
Germany	24	Sweden	12
Greece	12	UK	24
Ireland	9		

The function of the Committee is to advise the Council and the Commission and to prepare opinions on matters that it thinks are important in the economic and social fields.

Members of the Committee are appointed for four years by the Council of Ministers from a cross-section of the general public nominated by member states. The Committee elects its own Chair who holds office for two years.

The Maastricht Treaty, without giving explicit additional powers to the Committee, does provide that it shall be consulted by the Council and Commission on those matters where the scope of the Community is extended such as trans-European networks, consumer protection, etc.

The Regional Committee

The Regional Committee was established in 1975 as a means of promoting the development of the poorer and usually less geographically-accessible regions of the community. The Committee comprises senior civil servants from member states with administrative support from the Commission. The Committee operates the Regional Development Fund and, under the provision of the Maastricht Treaty, is entitled to be consulted on such matters as trans-European networks.

The European Investment Bank

The European Investment Bank (EIB) was created by Articles 129 and 130 of the Treaty of Rome. Its headquarters are in Luxembourg. Its members are the 15 member states.

Composition

The Board of Governors consists of one minister from each member state. It meets once a year.

The Board of Directors consists of members nominated by individual states and meets at least 12 times a year. It has responsibility for approving loans and the terms of those loans.

The Management Committee makes recommendations to the Board of Directors as to whether loans should be made and implements the Directors' decisions. It is responsible for the day-to-day running of the EIB.

Functions

Under Article 130 of the Treaty, the EIB is empowered to ensure 'the balanced and steady development of the Community' by means of providing loans or loan guarantees to member states for projects which will enable individual member states to work towards EU goals. It operates on a non-profit making basis.

Certain conditions have to be met before the EIB will grant loan finance:

- The loan must in some way contribute to economic growth in one or more of the poorer members of the EU
- Whilst contributing to economic growth, it must also assist in enabling the Union as a whole to work towards the accomplishment of common policy, e.g. transport/energy objectives
- It must also contribute towards enhancing the competitiveness of EU industry
- In financial terms, the project must not be expected to make a loss. There must be provision of adequate security so that in the event of the project not being successful, the EIB does not incur losses. Interest rates are lower than ruling market rates, thereby encouraging investment in projects with relatively low rates of return

The EIB obtains its loan capital from two sources: contributions from EU members and the financial markets.

Its activities (loan making) have been extended to include outside member countries to comply with cooperation agreements with countries in the Mediterranean region, central and eastern Europe, Latin America, Asia and the ACP countries.

The Institutions of the Union ... What Next?

The institutions are well established and have been refined as new members joined the union. Students may wish to consider:

– Could the institutions continue in their current format should the union increase its membership?

– Is there an argument for increasing the power of the European parliament?

– Could the decision-making process be improved in any way?

5 European Union Law

This chapter covers:

★ The distinction between procedural law and substantive law
★ The distinction between Union law and domestic (or national) law
★ The relationship between Union law and British domestic law
★ The nature of sovereignty
★ When individuals may have recourse to Union law in a national court: 'direct effect'
★ 'Secondary' legislation: regulations, directives and decisions
★ The operation of the European Court of Justice

Introduction: Some Distinctions

European Union law is a complicated area and it can seem difficult to explain any one of the fundamental concepts without referring to others equally in need of explanation. However, before any understanding of EU law can be reached, it is essential to grasp some basic distinctions, namely between:

• procedural and substantive law
• Union and domestic (or national) law
• primary and secondary law

Procedural Law and Substantive Law

• Procedural laws are those which relate to how law is made, how legal rules relate to each other, how they work and how they are applied
• Substantive laws are those which give effect to the policy decisions of the legislators

The law of the European Union contains both procedural and substantive elements. The Treaties that establish what the Union is and how it works, that set up the constitution of the Union and define the relationships between the Union as an institution and the member states, constitute procedural law. The rules that set out in detail what Union policies are in various areas and how they are to implemented in the member states, constitute substantive law.

Community Law and National Law

The laws of the European Union, as created by the Treaties and related Union legislation, are distinct from the body of law enacted by the legislature of each individual member state. This latter is called either 'national law' or 'domestic law'.

We shall see below that there are areas in which the relative priority of Union and national law becomes a matter for dispute. None the less, the possibility of such conflict does not arise in all areas of public and private life: while national law may from time to time have to be changed by the governments of the member states to bring it into line with Union law, there are many areas of national law that remain relatively untouched by a country's membership of the EU. Criminal law and matrimonial law are two examples of this.

Primary and Secondary Legislation

Many textbooks divide Union laws into primary and secondary legislation: the Treaty provisions that establish the legal framework of the Union and set out its basic policies and principles of operation are primary legislation, whereas the rules of various kinds by which those policies are implemented are secondary legislation.

This is a useful way of classifying Union law, and one that is used in this chapter. However, it is essential to grasp that no hierarchical distinction is involved; that is, secondary legislation is in no way inferior to or less powerful than primary legislation.

A Cautionary Note!

It is important not to confuse primary and secondary sources of European Union law with procedural and substantive law. The primary sources of law are, as we have said, contained in the Treaties, mainly the Treaty of Rome and its subsequent amendments. But the rules contained here are not all procedural. Article 199, for example, provides that men and women shall receive equal pay for equal work. This is a substantive legal rule.

Similarly, directives and regulations, secondary sources of law, may lay down procedural rules; for example, Directive 76/207, which guarantees equal treatment, requires member states to exercise their rights via due process of law. In other words, to give individuals rights of access to the courts, if necessary, to challenge any failure to implement the legal rule concerned.

Primary Legislation: The Treaties

The Treaties are usually referred to as primary sources of law, in the sense that although they do not for the most part contain detailed legal rules, they are where we find the basic legal principles of the Community. The Treaties which make up the Union (see below) can be thought of as the Union's constitution; they state what the major policies of the Community are and they establish in broad terms by what means those policies can be put into practice.

THE UNION TREATIES

The Treaty of Rome, 1957
The Merger Treaty, 1965
The Acts of Accession of the various member states, UK: 1972
Budgetary Treaties, 1970 and 1975
The Single European Act, 1986
The Treaty on European Union (The Maastricht Treaty, 1992)
The Treaty of Amsterdam, 1997

Union Law and Domestic Law

In order for a country to join the European Union, its head of state must sign the Treaty of Rome. However, when a sovereign state signs an international treaty it does not necessarily follow that the provisions of that treaty automatically become part of the domestic law of that state; that is, they cannot necessarily be enforced in the national courts of that state.

Dualism

The UK constitution regards international law and domestic law as two entirely separate legal systems. The subjects of international law are sovereign states; the subjects of domestic law are individuals. According to this theory, individuals cannot be the subject of international law. This approach is called 'dualism', and is adhered to by the UK.

For example, the European Convention on Human Rights (an international treaty) was signed by the UK in 1950. It has never been enacted by the British parliament as a national law. It is therefore not possible for an individual to stand up in a domestic court in the UK and claim his or her rights under the Convention directly. If there is no remedy under any domestic legal rule to help, the only redress is to the European Court of Human Rights (not to be confused with the European Court of Justice), the authority set up by the Convention with jurisdiction in the area of human rights.

SOVEREIGNTY: WHAT IS IT?

What is a sovereign state?

A sovereign state is one which has the power to make its own legal rules and political decisions without reference to any other controlling state. Like individuals, sovereign states may voluntarily enter agreements which may limit their powers to act as they wish.

What is parliamentary sovereignty?

Parliamentary sovereignty is the right of the legislature (parliament) to make and repeal whatever legal rules it wishes. The UK constitution does not allow for any parliament to pass a legal rule which cannot in theory be replaced by any subsequent parliament.

When a national legislature passes a law that cannot be repealed in the normal way, it is said to have 'entrenched' that piece of legislation. This is a procedure often used by those countries with written constitutions. It ensure that changing a constitutional rule is a more serious and more difficult step than to change an 'ordinary' piece of legislation.

The European Communities Act 1972: 'Hooking In' the Treaty of Rome

Because of Britain's adherence to dualism and in order for the Treaty of Rome to be made part of domestic law in the UK, it was necessary for the UK to pass a domestic Act of Parliament. This was the European Communities Act of 1972. This piece of legislation can be regarded as a 'hook' which brings the Treaty of Rome into national law.

Section 2(1) of the European Communities Act 1972, which gives effect to the Treaty of Rome in UK law, reads as follows:

> All such rights, powers, liabilities, obligations and restrictions from time to time created or arising by or under the Treaties, or in accordance with the Treaties, are without further enactment to be given legal effect or used in the UK and shall be recognised and available in law and shall be enforced, allowed and followed accordingly; and the expression 'enforceable Community right' and similar expressions shall be read as referring to one to which this subsection applies.

It is important to understand, however, that the European Communities Act is only an ordinary Act of Parliament, just like any other. It has not been 'entrenched' (see box above) – indeed, there is no means of doing this in the UK constitution.

From a strictly legal point of view, therefore, the Act can be repealed with as much ease as, say, the Road Traffic Act. That doesn't mean, of course, that there wouldn't be enormous political and economic obstacles to repealing the Act, but in theory it could be done.

To Recap ...

So, if we sum up at this point, we find:

- That according to UK law, only states (and some international organisations) – not individuals – are the subjects of international law
- That in order to become a member of the European Union, a member state must sign the Treaty of Rome and go through any procedures required by its own constitution to bring the provisions of the Treaty into domestic law
- That even after the Treaty of Rome was implemented in UK law by the passing of the European Communities Act, it is not the case that all the provisions of the Treaty can be claimed by individuals in domestic courts; they cannot. However, some provisions of the Treaty of Rome do give rights to individuals which can be claimed in national courts (this point is discussed in more detail below)
- That in effect, therefore, the European Union has created a set of legal rules which are both (a) international and bind member states on the one hand, and (b) domestic and bind and give rights to individuals on the other

In an early case (*Costa* v. *ENEL* – Case 6/64 1964 (ECR) 585) the European Court of Justice had this to say about Union law and its relationship with domestic law:

> By contrast with ordinary international treaties the EEC Treaty has created its own legal system, which on the entry into force of the Treaty, becomes an integral part of the legal systems of the member states and which their courts are bound to apply. By creating a community of unlimited duration having ... powers stemming from a limitation of sovereignty, or a transfer of powers from the states to the Community, the member states have limited their sovereign rights, albeit with limited fields, and have thus created a body of law which binds both their nationals and themselves.

Two further questions immediately arise:

- What is the relationship between European Union laws on the one hand and domestic laws on the other, and what happens in the event of a conflict between the two?

- Can individuals claim rights given by the Treaties in national courts and how do we know which these rights are?

Community Law and Domestic Law: Which Takes Priority?

Article 5 of the Treaty of Rome states:

> Member states shall take all appropriate measures, whether general or particular, to ensure fulfillment of the obligations arising out of this Treaty or resulting from action taken by the institutions of the Community. They shall facilitate the achievement of the Community's tasks.
>
> They shall abstain from any measure which would jeopardise the attainment of the objectives of this Treaty.

In addition, S.2(4) of the European Communities Act 1972, speaks of giving effect to any enactment (of the Community) passed *or to be passed*.

All of this would seem to indicate that in effect the law-making power of future UK parliaments was limited in 1972 by the then parliament and that law making from that date must be construed in the light of Union law. We can see how this takes place in practice by studying the examples of *Garland* v. *British Rail Engineering* and the Spanish Fisheries cases (see boxes). The former demonstrates that the UK courts may interpret UK law to conform to Union law. The latter demonstrated not only that the UK courts have the power to interpret UK law so that it does not conflict with Union law, but that they can actually suspend Acts of Parliament which do conflict. It is therefore apparent that parliament's law-making capacity has indeed been limited by membership of the Union.

On the other hand, should parliament wish to withdraw from the Union, then the European Communities Act 1972 could be repealed. It might help to imagine the situation as similar to that when a person joins a club, agreeing as a condition of admittance not to do anything now or in the future which conflicts with membership, but not thereby giving away the right to leave the club if so desired. Preliminary sovereignty is suspended but not given away.

GARLAND v. BRITISH RAIL ENGINEERING, 1982

Article 119 of the Treaty of Rome includes a framework for an entitlement to special travel facilities for former employees after retirement, even in the absence of a formal contractual entitlement. The UK Equal Pay Act 1970 makes no such provision. The House of Lords ruled that the provisions of this Act must be interpreted to conform with Article 119.

THE SPANISH FISHERIES CASE

In 1988, the UK parliament passed the Merchant Shipping Act. The aim of this Act was to safeguard the British inshore fishing fleet. The Union's common fisheries policy sets strict catch quotas for each national fishing fleet and Spanish owners were registering their vessels as British in order to gain a share in the British quota. The Act attempted to prevent registration as British any fishing vessel owned by a foreign national. Some 95 Spanish trawlers were affected.

One of the cornerstones of union policy is the freedom of establishment, which gives every Union national the right to establish him – or herself – as a self-employed person in another member state. The Act effectively prevented non-UK nationals from setting up in business as trawler operators in the UK.

Owners of the Spanish vessels unable to register under the new legislation challenged its validity. Using the Article 177 procedure (see page 144), the matter was referred to the European Court of Justice.

Pending the result of their hearing, however, a dispute arose as to whether in the meantime the Spanish vessels could continue to fish. The House of Lords (the UK's highest court) had to decide whether or not it could temporarily suspend the operation of the Merchant Shipping Act, pending the European Court of Justice's judgement. This in turn became a matter for the European Court of Justice, which held that the House of Lords could suspend the law.

The Merchant Shipping Act was repealed, in part as a result of an action by the Commission against the UK government.

Individuals and Community Law: 'Direct Effect'

The second question we identified is whether, as the Treaty of Rome has been 'hooked' into national law, an individual citizen can go to a national court and claim his rights under the Treaty. Not all provisions of the Treaty give such individual rights; those which can be used in this way are said to have 'direct effect'.

The European Court of justice decided in 1962 that some provisions of the Treaty of Rome do have direct effect, and in the case of *Van Gend en Loos* (Case 26/62) it set out the test which determines whether an individual treaty provision is directly effective. In order to have direct effect, a treaty provision must be:

- clear and unambiguous
- unconditional
- capable of taking effect without further action by either the Community or a member state

This rule has proved valuable in many situations where individuals have felt that their rights, e.g. as to free movement or equal treatment, have been infringed, and it has given them a way of claiming their rights in their own domestic courts (see following box for example).

Treaty provisions are sometimes stated to have 'horizontal' or 'vertical direct effect'. This is less confusing than it sounds. Treaty provisions may impose obligations on member states which can be enforced against that member state by an individual; these provisions are said to have *vertical* direct effect. Treaty provisions may create rights which an individual can claim against another individual; these provisions are said to have *horizontal* direct effect.

DEFRENNE v. *SABENA* (No. 2) (CASE 43/75)

Article 119 of the Treaty of Rome is the equal treatment provision. It provides that men and women should receive equal pay for equal work.

The reasoning behind this is not only that of social equality, but also that member states and companies which implement equal pay should not be at a competitive disadvantage compared to those member states and organisations where it is not implemented.

Miss Defrenne sued her former employers, the Belgian airline Sabena for compensation following their failure to pay air hostesses and cabin stewards equally.

The provisions of Article 199 comply with the test in *Van Gend en Loos* and have direct effect. Miss Defrenne's claim in her own national court was therefore successful.

These two European cases which establish the existence of vertical and horizontal direct effect are the two already mentioned in this section.

In *Van Gend en Loos* (Case 26/62), the Court established that the actions of the Dutch public authorities could be challenged by an individual company in respect of customs duty placed on glue. This is vertical direct effect.

Defrenne v. *Sabena* (No. 2) (Case 43/75), set out in the previous box shows an individual claiming rights under the Treaty against another individual. This is horizontal direct effect.

Secondary Legislation: Regulations, Directives, Decisions

It is through so-called 'secondary' legislation that the European Union puts into place the thousands of detailed rules which are necessary for the operation of the Community and the single market. It is also through the secondary legislation that the domestic laws of member states are harmonised where this is deemed to be important or necessary for the operation of the Union.

The powers of the various bodies which make secondary legislation and the way that legislation operates, derives from the Treaties. If the Treaties are the primary source of Community law, then it does make logical sense to call the implementing rules secondary legislation; but it is essential to remember that secondary legislation is no less important or less powerful than primary legislation.

The three different types of secondary legislation are regulations, directives and decisions. We need to deal with each of them in turn.

Regulations

Article 189 of the Treaty of Rome states:

> A regulation shall have general application. It shall be binding in its entirety and directly applicable in all member states.

This means that once a regulation is issued it immediately and automatically becomes part of the law of every member state. This is sometimes referred to as being 'directly applicable'. A member state does not need to pass an Act of Parliament, or equivalent, to make a regulation part of its domestic law. A regulation is therefore a very powerful instrument of Union law-making, operating like a missile, bypassing the member state's own law-making process and penetrating the domestic law of that state.

Regulations may give individuals rights which can be enforced against other individuals and against member states.

Example

Regulation 1390/81 has the effect of coordinating the social security schemes of member states so that a contribution made in one member state counts when a claim is made in a different member state. This would give an individual claimant the right to enforce his claim in a domestic court where this was necessary.

Directives

Article 189 of the Treaty of Rome states:

> A directive shall be binding as to the result to be achieved, upon each member state to which it is addressed, but shall leave to the national authorities the choice and form of methods.

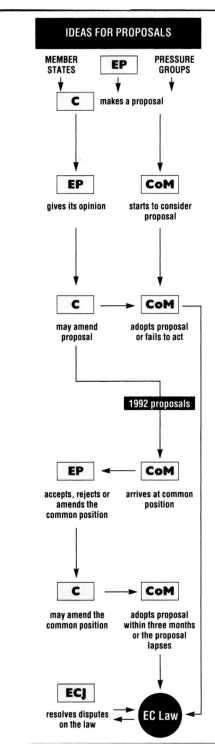

IDEAS FOR PROPOSALS

MEMBER STATES   EP   PRESSURE GROUPS

C makes a proposal

EP gives its opinion

CoM starts to consider proposal

C may amend proposal

CoM adopts proposal or fails to act

1992 proposals

EP accepts, rejects or amends the common position

CoM arrives at common position

C may amend the common position

CoM adopts proposal within three months or the proposal lapses

ECJ resolves disputes on the law

EC Law

STAGE 1
Ideas for laws can come from the Commission (C), the European Parliament (EP), national governments, and sometimes pressure groups. Only the Commission can decide which ideas to turn into 'proposals' for future laws. The draft proposal is written by the appropriate Directorate General. The Commission may consult on a draft proposal, say, with national civil servants, businesses and consumer representatives.

STAGE 2
The Council of Ministers (CoM) starts to consider the formal proposal. Meanwhile, in the EP, it is examined by the appropriate Committee. An MEP is appointed to prepare a report on the proposal and steer the discussion of it at the committee stage. The Committee's view is then presented for debate by all MEPs during a session of Parliament. At the end of the debate, the EP votes on its opinion of the proposal which will be put to the Council of Ministers via the Commission. The opinion of the EP can be to accept, amend, or refuse to approve a proposal.

STAGE 3
The Commission can ignore the opinion of the EP, but more often than not, the Commission will redraft the original proposal to reflect some or all of the EP's amendments. Amended proposals which are not part of the single market programme are sent to the Council of Ministers who either fail to act or adopt the proposal, in which case it becomes law, either as a regulation or as a directive. Proposals which do come under the single market programme go on to Stage 4.

STAGE 4
1992 or single market proposals are amended (or not) in the light of the EP's opinion and then sent to the Council of Ministers. The Council is bound to reach a 'common position' which means that the 12 member states have arrived at a version of the proposal that all, or a majority of them, can eventually accept. The common position then goes back to the EP for debate within three months. The EP has to give its opinion on whether to accept the Council's common position or to amend or reject it by absolute majority.

STAGE 5
The EP's opinion on the common position goes back to the Commission. It has one month to decide whether to amend the common position accordingly. The proposal then goes back to the Council who have three months in which to reach a decision (though they can ask the EP for a one month extension). If the Council agrees to the Commission's amended proposal, it can be adopted by a majority vote. If the Council wants to stick by the original common position, the proposal must be adopted by a unanimous vote.

Figure 5.1   How Union law is made

Source: Which?, June 1991

Directives are initially issued in draft form for consultation purposes, but once they are agreed, member states are usually given a time limit within which to implement them. How a member state implements a directive is a matter for that member state, as long as the desired result is obtained.

Example

Directive 85/374 was implemented by the UK parliament in 1987 when it passed the Consumer Protection Act 1987, which imposes strict liability on the producers of defective products.

In the historical case of *Francovich and Bonifaci* v. *Italy*, the European Court of Justice ruled that the plaintiffs were entitled to compensation from their own government as a result of that government's failure to implement EC Directive 80/987, which provided for compensation to be paid following an employer's bankruptcy. And in *Marshall* v. *Southampton Area Heath Authority*, the Court held that a government could not, as employer, take advantage of its own failure to implement a directive. *Francovich and Bonifaci* v. *Italy* extends this principle out of the public sector and provides that governments may have to pay compensation to any citizen or undertaking who loses out as a result of inability to claim in national court because of a non-implemented directive.

These decisions will act as a powerful incentive to member states not to lag behind in the implementation of directives; many cases have been brought since Francovich and Bonifaci, which will increase the rate at which member states implement directives.

Decisions

Article 189 of the Treaty of Rome states:

> A decision shall be binding in its entirely upon those to whom it is addressed.

Decisions are likely to be issued in relation to an individual member state, individual or organisation.

Example

The Commission may decide, on application from an individual company, whether a cooperation agreement it has made with another company infringes Union competition law.

The European Court of Justice

The job of the European Court of Justice is to ensure that the rules of the Union are adhered to by individuals, member states and other organisations of the Union. The Court decides what the relevant rules of Community law are and applies them where disputes arise between any of the bodies mentioned above.

A further task of the Court is to interpret the Treaties so that member states can ensure that decisions taken in national courts are taken in accordance with Union law. This is extremely important because:

1   The Treaties create what amounts to a new body of law; one that is partly international because it binds states, and partly national because it also binds individuals and can be implemented in national courts. The final arbiter of what those rules are, has to be a body which is supranational and has authority to ensure its decisions are adhered to.

2   It would lead to chaos if the courts and governments of members states were each to interpret the Treaties in their own way, so that there were many different interpretations of the Treaties in existence at any one time. This point is further complicated by the fact that the Treaty of Rome exists in many member states only in translation, and questions of interpretation are bound to arise.

Article 177

Article 177 of the Treaty of Rome gives the national courts of member states the power to refer cases to the European Court of Justice for a preliminary ruling on the meaning of any provision of the Treaty. The Court makes its interpretation and then refers it back to the national court, which proceeds to decide the case in accordance with the interpretation.

The European Court of Justice does not decide the case itself; it confines itself to deciding on the meaning of the relevant Treaty provision. The case is suspended while the Court's ruling is awaited.

If the question is a very serious one and the case ends up in the highest domestic court available, such as the House of Lords in the UK, then that court has duty to refer the matter to the European Court of Justice, whose decision is binding on the domestic court; it *must* follow its interpretation.

British courts were initially reluctant to use this procedure, believing that their judges were capable of making decisions in accordance with Union law without the need for a referral. In recent years, however, it has been invoked much more frequently.

Example

In *Torfaen Borough Council* v. *B&Q Plc* (145/88) the Article 177 procedure was invoked to establish whether or not UK Sunday-trading laws contravened Article 30 of the Treaty of Rome. At that stage the Court decided that shop opening hours were possibly a restriction on trade which might be against Union law.

Unlike UK domestic courts, however, the European Court of Justice is not bound by any doctrine of precedent (i.e. it does not have to follow previous decisions). The House of Lords, therefore, decided to refer the matter to the European Court under Article 177 again and see if a different decision would be reached. The Court reported in December 1992 that restricting Sunday opening involved no contravention of EC law.

A Summary

What, then, can we conclude at the end of this brief outline of Union law?

- That Union law takes priority over national law
- That Union policies are implemented by secondary legislation
- That some provisions of the Treaty of Rome are directly effective and can be claimed as rights by individuals in national courts
- That parliamentary sovereignty has been limited by membership of the Union
- That where provisions of the Treaty need interpreting, the European Court of Justice may be called upon, using the procedure outlined in Article 177

European Law ... What Next?

The conflict between Union law and the domestic law of member countries is likely to be an issue for many years. Students should monitor examples of:

- Situations were a decision to vary Union law (perhaps through a directive) causes a problem or delay at British level.

- Cases where Union law does not conform with British law.

6 Freedom of Movement in the Single European Market

> **This chapter covers**
> ★ A review of progress towards implementation of the 'four freedoms'
> ★ Policy on the free movement of labour
> ★ Policy on the free movement of goods
> ★ Competition policy

The 'Four Freedoms'

The objective of creating a single 'common market' among the Community member states was explicitly set out in Article 2 of the Treaty of Rome:

> The Community shall have as its task by establishing a common market and progressively approximating the economic policies of member states, to promote throughout the Community a harmonious development of economic activities ...

Also enshrined in the Treaty, in pursuit of the objective of the common market, were the so-called 'four freedoms' (see Figure 6.1, page 148):

- the free movement of people
- the free movement of goods
- the free movement of services
- the free movement of capital

These were among the founding principles of the Community, on which its policies would be based.

The original six members of the Community had hoped to have implemented all the main aims of the founding Treaties within 12 years of their signature, and in particular by this time, to have created a single European economy with common policies in key areas.

However, while progress was rapid in some areas, e.g. the Common Agricultural Policy (see Chapter 8), it was very slow in others. Many of the original barriers to a single market remained, and new ones appeared. These included:

- the various obstacles to the free movement of people
- differing national technical specifications
- differing national health and safety standards

- differing national environmental regulations
- differing national quality controls

Together, these restrictions on economic activity in the EU were known as non-tariff barriers, and they constituted a formidable obstacle to achievement of the single market.

Economic integration was also complicated by the addition of new members to the Union with widely differing degrees of economic development and a variety of established national practices.

The Single European Act and the Single Market

In contrast to the vision of the Union's founders, by the early 1980s a true common market was still a long way from reality. This was ironic, as in the minds of most people this was the Union's central purpose.

The Single European Act of 1986 established a tight timetable for the achievement of an open economic system in Europe in which the four freedoms would be a practical reality. It defined the single market as:

> An area without internal frontiers in which the free movements of goods, persons, services and capital is ensured in accordance with the provisions of the Treaty

The Act decreed that by 1 January 1993, all barriers to such a single market should be lifted.

In the intervening six years, much work was done on the implications of the single market – and of failure to achieve it. In 1988, the Commission published *The European Challenge 1992: The Benefits of a Single Market* (popularly known as the Cecchini Report, after the chairman of the working party which produced it). This document estimated the costs to the industries within the Union of non-completion of the internal market and assessed the likely benefits of its achievement (see following box).

THE COSTS OF NON-EUROPE

- high administrative costs incurred in dealing with different national bureaucratic requirements
- higher transport costs because of formalities at borders
- increased costs as a result of having to apply different national standards and so having smaller product runs
- duplication of costs involved in separate research and development

---

- high costs of non-competitive and heavily-regulated state activities as exemplified by national public procurement policies
- high costs and reduced choice for consumers confined to their national markets
- the opportunity cost which prevents or discourages economic activity from spreading across frontiers to enjoy the full market potential

THE BENEFITS OF THE SINGLE MARKET

By 1988:
- a gain of about 4.5 per cent (£129 billion) in Community GDP
- a reduction in prices of 6 per cent
- the creation of 2 million extra jobs

Although 1 January 1993 did not see the lifting of a curtain on a new market similar in operation to that existing among the states of the USA, with each of the four freedoms at a different stage of development and progress towards a truly free market varying from one area to another, progress has been considerable.

PEOPLE

Border controls between most EC countries have vanished. Passport checks, where they exist, are lighter throughout the EC (see Schengen Agreement). New rules mean some qualifications are now recognised EC-wide, allowing people to work abroad more easily.

But, the UK retains border checks, emphasising the need to prevent smuggling, illegal immigration and rabies.

GOODS

Customs checks at borders between EC states have vanished; there is a new blue channel at customs, and millions of pages of customs forms have disappeared. Consumers can buy alcohol, tobacco and other produces for personal use effectively without restrictions on how much they can take home.

But, prices continue to vary widely as VAT has not been equalised. New VAT payments and trade statistics are handled by an EC-wide system which some businesses believe is too complicated. It is still harder to buy imported cars in some EC states than in others (see Competition Policy, page 154).

SERVICES

Lawyers, engineers, accountants, teachers, opticians and some others are allowed to practise in other EC countries. There will be a single banking licence and a similar scheme for insurance companies will be phased in.

But, in some areas, especially those connected with state ownership, such as telecommunications and broadcasting, there remain serious restrictions. In practice, there are still obstacles to selling other professional services across borders. Further information on banking and insurance will be found in Chapter 8.

CAPITAL

Citizens can borrow and save with EC banks which use their new freedom to do business outside their home state. Capital controls are lifted and business can invest freely throughout the EC.

But, some special exemptions remain. Above all, there continues to be costs for changing money since the Single European Act does not establish a common currency (see Chapter 7). Further information on banking and insurance will be found in Chapter 8.

Figure 6.1 The four freedoms

The remaining sections of this chapter will examine the Community's policy on the free movement of labour and goods.

Free Movement of Labour

The rules about free movement of labour are contained in Articles 48–58 of the Treaty of Rome.

KEY PROVISIONS OF THE TREATY OF ROME

Article 48
Article 48 states that freedom of movement for workers shall be secured within the Union, it abolishes discrimination based on nationality and gives member states the right to refuse entry to an applicant on the grounds that the personal conduct of an individual contravenes considerations of:

* public policy
* public security
* public health

> ### Article 51
> Article 51 provides the right for nationals of a member state who are self-employed to establish themselves in business in the territory of another member state.
>
> ### Article 11 (Regulation 1612/68)
> Article 11 provides that the family of the national of a member state has the right to accompany a worker when he takes up employment or establishes himself in another member state. Family members do not have to be EU nationals. Cohabitees in a stable relationship are included in this right. Cohabitees in same-sex relationships are not.

These provisions of the Treaty of Rome are supplemented by various regulations and directives and now by significant case law both in national courts and in the European Court of Justice.

Example: *Van Duyn* v. *Home Office* (Case 41/74) (1975) 2 WLR 760

In 1968, the UK government announced that it considered the Church of Scientology socially harmful in that it alienated families and damaged the psychological health of its followers. British immigration authorities refused to grant entry to Miss Van Duyn who had been given a job by the organisation.

Miss Van Duyn claimed in an English court that the ban was unlawful because it was a breach of Article 48 of the Treaty of Rome. On a reference to the European court of Justice under the Article 177 procedure, the court confirmed the exclusion on the grounds that Miss Van Duyn's current connection with the Church of Scientology amounted to unacceptable personal conduct and that there was a genuine and serious threat to one of the fundamental interests of society. All of the four freedoms are subject to limitations which enable states, for example, to prevent the entry of persons where public policy, public health or public security is at stake.

> ### THE SCHENGEN AGREEMENT
>
> The Schengen Agreement of March 1995 gives citizens of countries who have signed, the right to cross national borders only displaying a green sticker. No other identity document need be shown. Full signatories at the time of the Amsterdam Summit were Germany, France, Belgium, Luxembourg, Portugal, Spain and Holland. Italy, Austria, Greece, Denmark, Finland and Sweden have signed but have not yet fully implemented it.
>
> Britain and Ireland have not signed and retain an opt-out in recognition of their status as islands. Norway and Iceland, not EU members but sharing a passport-free union with the Scandinavian EU members, maintain cooperation accords with the Schengen area.

Free Movement of Goods

KEY PROVISIONS OF THE TREATY OF ROME

Article 9
The Community shall be based upon a customs union which shall cover all trade in goods, and which shall involve the prohibition between member states of customs duties on imports and exports and of all charges having equivalent effect, and the adoption of a common customs tariff in their relation with third countries.

Article 30
Quantitative restrictions on imports and all measures having equivalent effect shall ... be prohibited between member states.

Article 95
No member state shall impose directly or indirectly on the products of other member states, any internal taxation of any kind in excess of that imposed directly or indirectly on similar domestic products.

Example: *Rewe-Zentral AG* v. *Bundesmonopolverwaltung für Branntwein* (Case 120/78)

(Otherwise known as *Cassis de Dijon.*)
Cassis is a blackcurrant liqueur produced in both France and Germany. That produced in France has an alcohol level of 15–20 per cent. German regulations specified that spirits should have a 25 per cent alcohol level. This meant that French cassis could not be marketed in Germany as it did not reach the minimum alcohol requirement.

Under the Article 177 procedure, the European Court of Justice ruled that Article 30 of the Treaty of Rome had been breached by the German regulation. In reaching this decision the Court applied a test known as 'The Rule of Reason', which states that obstacles to free movement of goods which result from differences in national laws must go no further than is necessary to protect public health, consumers, commercial fairness or effective tax supervision. Any rules which, in effect, protect goods produced domestically against imported goods, shall be in breach of Article 30.

The Court also stated that goods which have been lawfully produced and marketed in one member state, cannot be prevented from entering another member state and being marketed there, unless the rule in the importing state which prohibits the importation and sale is deemed to be necessary to protect some legitimate interest.

This idea, that member states must recognise the legitimacy of product lawfully marketed in another member state, was of great assistance in the development of the Single European Market. It establishes the principle of mutual recognition as a possible alternative to the harmonisation of standards; a development which enabled the single market to be achieved more quickly than it otherwise would have been.

Free Movement of Services

The rules about free movement of services are contained in Articles 59–66 of the Treaty of Rome.

KEY PROVISIONS OF THE TREATY OF ROME

Article 59
Article 59 states that restrictions on freedom to provide services shall be abolished.

Article 60
Defined services as *including*:

- services of an industrial character
- activities of a commercial character
- activities of craftsmen
- activities of the professions

The wording of Article 60 here, obviously means that provision of other services may also fall within the scope of the Article.

Article 60 also provides that EU nationals who provide services in a member state shall be entitled to do so under the same conditions as nationals of that state.

Article 1(1) of Directive 73/48 also makes it clear that there shall be freedom for nationals of member states to go to another member state as a *recipient* of services. This would include, for example, tourists, students or persons seeking medical treatment.

It is also important to note under the provision of services that Article 7 of the Treaty of Rome provides that 'any discrimination on the grounds of nationality shall be prohibited'.

Freedom to provide services has to be seen in the context of freedom of establishment, the essential differences between the two being that, according to Article 60, freedom to provide services means services of a *temporary* nature. Permanent provision of a service in another member state is part of the right of freedom of establishment.

Competition Policy

Competition policy is a central component of the single market arrangements. In pursuit of the aim of preventing the erection of barriers to trade within the Union, it has three main objectives:

- To prevent companies from entering into price-fixing and market-sharing agreements
- To prevent anti-competitive practices which may result from market power being concentrated into the hands of monopoly, duopoloy or oligopoly
- To prevent national governments from distorting competition in the community by favouring national companies

---

KEY PROVISIONS OF THE TREATY OF ROME

Article 85
The following shall be prohibited as incompatible with the common market: all agreement between undertakings, decisions by association of undertakings and concerted practices which may affect trade between member states and which have as their object *or effect* the prevention, restriction or distortion of competition within the common market.

Article 86
Any abuse by one or more undertakings of a dominant position within the common market or in a substantial part of it shall be prohibited as incompatible with the common market in so far as it may affect trade between member states.

Articles 85 and 86 of the Treaty of Rome contain a broad statement of Union policy on competition. These provisions are reinforced by regulations as applied by the Commission and enforced by the European Court of Justice. Offending institutions can be ordered to terminate practices in contravention of Union rules and may be fined.

Example I: *Akzo Chemie BV* v. *Commission* (1987) ICMLR 231

Akzo, a producer of chemicals, undercut the prices of ECS, a small British company that wished to expand into Akzo's market.

The Commission held that Akzo's actions were an abuse of its dominant position in the market and not only discouraged ECS from competing, but also deterred other companies from competing against Akzo in the future.

Example 2: *Consten and Grundig* v. *Commission* (1966) ECR 299

This case concerned an exclusive dealing agreement between Grundig, a manufacturer in Germany, and Consten, a distributor in France.

A condition of Consten's being Grundig's exclusive distributor in France was that Consten would not export to any other member states goods which it had imported into France from Germany. The effect of this would be to restrict competition in France and other member states. The European Court held that such an agreement was a breach of Article 85.

Example 3: The Bosman Ruling

In 1995, the European Court of Justice ruled that the practices of UEFA (European Union of Football Associations) of (a) allowing clubs to charge a transfer fee for players whose contracts have run out and (b) allowing a maximum of three EU and two non-EU players in European games ran counter to EU competition rules. With regard to transfers, only those from one EU country to another were covered. The case had been brought by the Belgian footballer Jean-Marc Bosman.

Following this, in January 1996, the EU Competition Commissioner, in response to a request by UEFA for exemption, gave both UEFA and FIFA (the world body) six weeks to implement the Bosman ruling. It is worth noting that the European Court's ruling was based on contravention of EU rules on free movement of workers, whereas the later ruling was a competition issue. The Commission also indicated that it might act on transfers within national leagues.

Example 4: VAG in Italy

In early 1998, the Commission fined Volkswagen and its subsidiary Audi, Ecu 102 million for preventing its Italian dealers from selling cars to customers in Austria and Germany where the same vehicles were more expensive. Other car manufacturers are under scrutiny for similar contraventions. Evidence was presented of long-standing practices involving threats to withdraw concessions to dealers and pressurising the dealers to 'find pretexts for refusing to sell … (using) differences in the specifications and difficulties in upholding the guarantee' (European Commission ruling).

Freedom of Movement in the Single Market ... What Next?

Students should investigate, in the period up to and after the Millennium:

- The level of progress, in Union countries, of cross-border acceptance of professional qualifications.
- Any infringements of competition policy and how these are dealt with.

7 *Economic and Monetary Policy*

Introduction: Exchange Rate Policy in Europe

An important pillar of the single market is the concept of monetary union. As long ago as the late 1960s, it was recognised by the then member states of the Union that closer economic and monetary union was essential if the goals of the original Treaty of Rome were to be realised.

The then EEC or EC had no wish to repeat the economic mistakes of the inter-war period. During the 1920s and 1930s as world trade declined, those countries who relied very heavily on overseas trade for their markets found themselves competing for a steadily diminishing market. Competitive devaluations became the order of the day as each country tried to obtain a price advantage over its trade rivals. Any gains achieved in this way were very short-term, though, as rival countries devalued in turn in order to re-establish the original price relationships.

During this period, countries also used import quotas and tariffs to protect their own domestic goods from foreign competition. This protectionist approach, on top of the competitive devaluations, further decreased the level of foreign trade in real terms, thus only exacerbating the problem.

The Bretton Woods system: Fixed Exchange Rates

Only rearmament and the coming of the Second World War in 1939 broke the cycle, as countries' economies were revived with the demand for military goods and services. As the war seemed to be approaching its end, however, it was clear that new arrangements would have to be made to deal with the international economy. The Bretton Woods Conference of 1944 established the International Monetary Fund (IMF) and a return to a system of fixed exchange rates. This had applied under the Gold Standard which was abandoned in 1931. The IMF would ensure that member states maintained their respective exchange rates and that changes were agreed only if a member country had a persistent balance of payments surplus or deficit. Should a country's currency come under pressure in the foreign exchange market, that country could call on supplementary funds made available by the IMF to national central banks to support their currencies in such circumstances.

There are inherent difficulties in any fixed exchange-rate scheme, and these soon became apparent. (To some extent they have been reflected in the operation of the EMS: see page 160). Those countries with persistently high levels of inflation found this reflected in poor export performance and balance of payments deficits, because their exports were relatively expensive on the world market. Conversely, those countries with low levels of inflation, such as Japan and Germany, found themselves with regular balance of payments surpluses, because their exports were relatively cheap on the world market.

Countries that persistently operated a balance of payments deficit, could not maintain a fixed rate of exchange for an indefinite period of time as they lacked the necessary gold and convertible foreign-exchange reserves to maintain the par-value of their currency on the foreign exchange market. (Par-value was maintained by buying their own currency with gold and convertible foreign-exchange reserves that were earned when the balance of payments was in surplus.)

If a country permanently operated a balance of payments surplus or deficit, it was deemed to be in a state of 'fundamental disequilibrium' and speculators would therefore anticipate either a revaluation (balance of payments surplus) or devaluation (balance of payments deficit). In turn, the very buying or selling of the currency in question by speculators, made it inevitable that an exchange rate change would indeed occur.

The Bretton Woods system of fixed exchange rates, unable to cope with the stresses that had developed, collapsed in 1971. It was replaced by a system of floating rates, in which each currency's value against others is determined by the interaction of supply and demand on the international currency markets. The IMF remained in being with a modified role, no longer underpinning a fixed-rate system.

From the Werner Report to the European Monetary System

In October 1970 at a summit held at the Hague, Union leaders made the first moves towards recognising that the aims of the Treaty of Rome would not be met unless common, or at least coordinated, economic policies were brought into being. The leaders considered the report of a committee of financial and monetary experts, chaired by Luxembourg's Prime Minister, Pierre Werner. The Werner Report proposed:

- progressive unification of economic policies
- the establishment of common monetary policies, embracing capital movements, tax harmonisation and common budgetary policy, that would achieve, by 1980, a common EC currency and complete economic and monetary union

Out of the Werner Report emerged what was eventually to become the European Monetary System (EMS).

The EMS has three main objectives:

- to reduce exchange rate fluctuation between member state currencies
- to reduce the currency uncertainties involved with inter-member trade and thereby increase trade, economic growth and employment
- 'establishment by stages of economic and monetary union in the Community'

One of the recommendations of the Werner Report was the establishment of the European Monetary Cooperation Fund (EMCF). This body was founded in 1973. As with the IMF and the Bretton Woods system, the EMCF plays an important role in the operation of the EMS and is seen by some as being an embryonic European Central Bank. The EMCF issues European Currency Unites (Ecus) to the central banks of member states in exchange for gold and convertible currencies.

April 1972 saw the establishment of the European Community currency 'snake'. This was the forerunner of the present Exchange Rate Mechanism (ERM). Just like ERM, its main role was to limit fluctuations in exchange rates between member state currencies. However, its success was limited; the UK's membership, for example, lasted only three months. By 1978, it was recognised that a more enduring system needed to be designed. In December 1978, agreement was reached on the EMS in the form in which it now exists. The EMS replaced the 'snake' in March 1979.

The EMS in Operation

The Advantages of Membership

The European Monetary System is seen as an important mechanism for achieving the aim of European monetary union by 1999 (see page 163). Under the EMS, not only the currencies of member states are joined, but also their economies.

Member states saw several related advantages in belonging to the ERM. The most important gains to members were seen to be:

- the movement towards low inflation
- the growth in trade between members resulting from lower levels of inflation
- economic growth and lower levels of unemployment resulting in turn from the growth in trade

Governments also saw the EMS as an opportunity to create an area of monetary stability between the currencies of EC member states, especially important in view of the fact that inter-EC trade accounts for a significant large proportion of many member states' exports.

So important was the EMS considered to be in underpinning the original objectives of the Treaty of Rome that it formed an integral part of the Single European Act of 1986 (see Chapter 3). The role and importance of the EMS were further enhanced after 1 January 1993 when the Single European Market (SEM) came into full effect, which in turn put further pressure on moves towards a full European Monetary Union.

Operational decisions concerning the EMS are the result of collective agreement between member state central banks and their respective Finance Ministers. Each of these two groups meets regularly, and since 1994 the European Monetary Institute (EMI) has been involved (see page 172).

How the Exchange Rate Mechanism Works

Each member state's currency enters the ERM at an agreed exchange rate against the Ecu. All the member states' currencies are weighted against it according to their various strengths. The exchange rate at which a member state's currency enters the ERM is set by the governors of the other member states' central banks and their respective Finance Ministers. As the German Deutschmark was the strongest of all the EU currencies in terms of low inflation and interest rates, some member states who joined the ERM additionally 'pegged' their currencies to the Deutschmark.

Britain joined the ERM in October 1990, at the same time as the

Spanish peseta; sterling was pegged to the Deutschmark at a rate of DM 2.95 to the pound. A condition of entry for both Britain and Spain was that their respective currencies were allowed a float of plus or minus 6 per cent either side of the agreed entry rate. Other member countries operated a plus or minus fluctuation of 2.25 per cent. The current allowed fluctuation is 15 per cent except between the Dutch guilder and the German Deutschmark where it is 2.25%.

WHAT IS THE ECU?

- The denominator of the ERM
- The unit of account for the intervention mechanisms of the ERM
- A measure of the divergence of currencies from their central rates within the EMS
- The reserve instrument for member states' central banks and the unit of exchange of inter-bank settlements between member states
- From 1999 (under present plans), the common European currency, but re-named the 'Euro'

There are 'intervention points' at the upper and lower limits of each country's exchange rates beyond which the central bank of that country must intervene to restore it to the agreed band. For example, a member country's currency may come under pressure in the foreign exchange markets due to a large balance of payments deficit or high levels of inflation in comparison to other member states. This pressure may be forcing the currency to the floor of its 15 per cent float.

In this case the central bank would be required to buy its currency in the foreign exchange market using its reserves of convertible currencies (e.g. dollar, yen, franc); if the currency were approaching the upper limit, it would be required to sell. Should support be required on a larger scale, central banks of other member states may be asked to participate in either buying or selling as appropriate.

The EMS has, in addition, created specific credit systems to which member states' central banks have access and which can be called upon for intervention purposes. These systems are known as VSTF or 'very short-term financing' facilities. Credit is available for a three-month period, after which it must normally be repaid, although it is possible for some of the borrowings to be carried forward for another three months. After this second period there can be no subsequent extension. VSTF is available only when it is necessary to finance 'obligatory intervention'; that is, when the currency in question is at the margins of its permissible range. VSTF finance operates via the EMCF.

In addition, or as an alternative to these options within the EMS, the government whose currency is under pressure may resort to domestic monetary policy controls, in particular, changes in interest rates.

In the event of either or both of these approaches failing, the member state faces two policy alternatives:

1 Firstly, it may seek approval for a realignment of its exchange rate against other member currencies away from its ERM entry rate. If there are upward pressures forcing the exchange rate towards the top of the band it can revalue, if it is at the bottom it can devalue. An individual member state cannot unilaterally decide to realign its currency; agreement much be reached with all other EMS states. In order to avoid currency speculation, such meetings and announcements are formally made at the weekend at a time when the foreign exchange markets are closed.

2 Secondly, and more drastically, it can temporarily leave the ERM. This option was taken by the UK government in September 1992 when the costs of supporting the pound (estimated at £1.8 billion) and temporary increases in interest rates to 15 per cent were ineffective in reversing the decline of the pound's value against other EU currencies. The British government and the Bank of England realised that there was no alternative to letting sterling find its own level on the foreign exchange markets. January 1993, likewise, saw Irish short-term overnight interest rates rise from 50 per cent to 100 per cent, forcing the government to devalue the punt.

The European Exchange Rate Mechanism is recognised as being far from perfect. It is a halfway house between a fixed and a floating exchange-rate system and is consequently vulnerable to speculative attacks. An obvious problem for the UK government, business organisations and individuals alike is that the UK economy was not been able to spend its way out of the early 1990s recession, for such action would probably have forced the pound towards the lower end its band.

A fundamental problem facing all parties to the existing ERM is that there is no formal mechanism to share out amongst members the costs of defending a currency which comes under pressure; at present the task falls solely upon the central bank of the country involved.

It is for these reasons that the EU is striving, via the Maastricht Treaty, to achieve total European Monetary Union with a European Central Bank and one common European currency, the Euro, by 1999.

European Monetary Union

The Delors Report

In 1988, the Delors Committee was established, with the task of proposing stages by which Economic and Monetary Union (EMU) might be achieved. EMU as to be based on strict economic principles that would have to be observed by member states. Members could be part of this Union only if they could prove that they had achieved stated standards of economic performance.

In 1989, the Delors Committee published its Report. It set out three stages by which EMU is to be arrived at.

Stage One

Stage One is centred on working towards the ratification by all member states of the Maastricht Treaty. The Maastricht Treaty is crucial to any further progress with EMU, for it created 'new' EU institutions that would achieve the objects of Stages Two and Three. During this stage, launched under EU powers already in existence, member states are to work more closely together in integrating their economic and monetary policies. Once the Maastricht Treaty has been ratified by all member states, Stage Two commences. Stage Two started on 1 January 1994.

Stage Two

The second stage involves the further harmonisation of policies regarding interest rates, exchange rates and monetary policy in preparation for the transition to the final stage, Stage Three. From the beginning of 1994, signatories of the Maastricht Treaty initiated the processes that led to the eventual independence of their national central banks from government control and influence. Also during 1994, the European Monetary Institute was established as the forerunner of the European Central Bank, which will come into operation under Stage Three.

Stage 3

At the Madrid Summit (December 1995) the Heads of State reconfirmed that Stage Three would begin on 1 January 1999. Agreement was reached on 'Euro' as the name of the single currency.

State Three will see the adoption of a common EU monetary policy and establishment of a European Central Bank working with the European System of Central Banks. The currencies of the member states will be fixed permanently in relation to each other and those that meet the convergence criteria will be replaced by a single common European currency, the Euro. The Euro will be a currency in its own right.

However, even when EMU is achieved, member countries and firms will not be able to ignore currency fluctuations altogether, having to take into account the exchange rate of the European Euro with other international currencies and trading blocks.

EMU: THE DELORS REPORT, 1989

Stage One:
from 1 July 1990

Establishment by 1 January 1993 of a Single European Market in:

• free movement of goods, services, labour and capital

• linkage of member states' currencies via the European Monetary System (EMS)

Establishment of Exchange Rate Mechanism (ERM) to which all member states belong.

Currency fluctuations to be ±2.25 per cent against the Ecu and each other.

Stage Two:
from 1 January 1994

Movement towards the harmonisation of:

• interest rates
• exchange rates
• monetary policies
• closer currency
• fluctuation bands

Establishment by 1 January 1994 of European Monetary Institute (EMI), forerunner of European Central Bank (ECB)

Process leading to the eventual independence of member state central banks from government control to begin.

European System of Central Banks established by July 1998, superseding the EMI.

Stage Three:
from 1 January 1999

Member countries' exchange rates fixed permanently. Establishment of a single European currency, the Ecu, by 1 January 1999.

Establishment of Common Monetary Policy.

Establishment of a European Central Bank to:

• define and implement Community monetary policy

• conduct foreign exchange operations

• hold and manage official foreign-exchange reserves of member states

---

The Maastricht Treaty

The Maastricht Treaty of 7 February 1992, was signed by the then 12 nations of the European Community at the conclusion of the summit held at Maastricht in Holland. This summit was a major event in the history of what is now called the European Union and

was part of the run-up to the implementation of the Single
European Act on 1 January 1993.

In terms of economic and monetary policy (the Treaty also
covered a wide range of other issues) the aim of Maastricht was to
establish a system of fixed exchange rates under the ERM,
following by a period where economic convergence between
member states would lead to full monetary union.

The Convergence Criteria

As a result of Maastricht, the term 'convergence' entered the
catalogue of European buzz-words along with the likes of
'subsidiarity' and 'Qualified Majority Voting'. 'Convergence'
means that member states must have broadly similar economies
before they can come together in a system of Economic and
Monetary Union (EMU). The official Maastricht convergence
criteria for a country to qualify were:

- **Inflation**
  – no more than 1.5 per cent above the average of the lowest
  three rates in the European Union
- **Exchange rates**
  – a stable exchange rate to be achieved. Within ERM bands for
  the previous two years
- **Government finances**
  – the budget deficit should be no greater than 3 per cent of
  gross domestic product and government debt should be within
  60 per cent of GDP
- **Interest rates**
  – there should not be more than 2 per cent above the average
  rate on government bonds in the three member countries with
  the lowest interest rates

Much has been made of the above criteria and periodically the
financial press attempts to assess the likelihood of Britain meeting
the criteria in the light of her current performance. The criteria are
probably best regarded as guidelines; those countries keenest on
joining a single currency are likely to argue for flexibility.
Satisfactory overall economic performance and closeness to
satisfying the criteria will count heavily.

Britain's performance judged against the criteria has proved
perhaps surprisingly, good. An assessment by the *Daily Telegraph*
in 1995, concluded that Britain, along with Germany and
Luxembourg, was likely to be one of only three countries meeting
the criteria by 1997. Britain had not, however, rejoined the ERM
by early 1998. Tables 7.1 and 7.2 show Britain's comparative
position in the key areas of inflation and government debt as a

percentage of GDP. Long-term interest rates tend to shadow the expected inflation rate, so this criterion also looks satisfactory.

Table 7.1:	Inflation – change in consumer prices			
	UK	Germany	France	Italy
1991	4.5	3.5	3.2	6.5
1992	2.6	4.0	2.4	5.3
1993	1.9	4.0	2.1	4.2
1994	2.9	2.7	1.7	4.6
1995	3.2	1.8	1.7	5.7
1996	2.5	1.5	2.0	3.9(F)
1997	3.4(F)	1.9(F)	1.3(F)	2.0(F)
1998	3.4(F)	2.4(F)	1.8(F)	2.5(F)

F = Forecast

Source: *Barclay's Country Reports*

Table 7.2:	National debt as % of GDP			
	UK	Germany	France	Italy
1991	36	43	41	100
1992	42	44	46	108
1993	45	52	46	118
1994	52	52	48	124
1995	55	62	53	123
1996	54	61	57	121

Source: *Barclay's Country Reports*

Why convergence criteria are necessary

As long as countries have control over their own exchange rates they have a powerful economic weapon. A country with a balance of payments deficit (where the value of its imports exceeds the value of its exports) may devalue its currency, ensuring that it is worth less in terms of other currencies. This will make its exports cheaper and imports dearer and thereby tend to reduce the deficit. Only if economies are sufficiently similar, i.e. have converged, can this weapon be regarded as potentially superfluous. It is worth considering, however, whether convergence at entry to a single currency implies continued convergence. The mere fact that the members of a single currency cannot suffer a conventional balance of payment deficit, because they will not have imports and exports valued in different currencies, is not important. The crucial factor is that if, for example, Britain was importing a much greater value of German goods than vice versa, she would be likely to suffer job losses and be unable to correct this by devaluation.

Even more important is the question of interest rates. Interest rates are actively used in a modern economy to control the level of economic activity, particularly inflation. Countries which are members of a single currency will not have independent control over their interest rates. This is because of the connection between interest rates and the exchange rate. If Britain raises its interest rates to curb inflation, the side effect will be to draw in foreign funds seeking a home with a relatively high return. This flow of foreign currency into sterling will strengthen the pound. If, under a single currency, a member country was allowed to unilaterally change its interest rates, there would be a flow of foreign funds into the single currency and this would alter the exchange rate of the single currency against foreign currencies (US dollar, yen, etc.). Clearly this would be unacceptable to a Central European Bank with an exchange rate target for the Single European Currency. It is vital, therefore, that member countries of the single currency should have convergent interest rates, but, again, it is not obvious that convergence at entry implies that there might not be a case for subsequent divergence.

A more sophisticated approach to the problems of joining (as opposed to merely meeting or not meeting convergence criteria) involves considering the fact that different economies operate in different economic cycles. For example, when the UK economy might be tending to overheat with increasing activity and inflationary pressures, that of France might be edging in a recessionary direction.

Figure 7.3, page 168, shows output gaps (the differences between potential and actual output) in a number of EU countries. The Netherlands, Finland and Ireland show considerable potential for overheating with excess actual output being translated into inflation. This is particularly the case in the Netherlands where the supply of labour is tight. The situation would demand higher interest rates compared to other countries where actual output is below potential. If you consider that the Netherlands and Germany have had their currencies closely tied for a number of years, it looks even more alarming. Table 7.3 shows their economies as markedly divergent, with a case for different interest rate strategies.

Finally there is the question of inequality. Figure 7.4 (page 169) shows changes in inequality in the EU during the 1980s. Inequality between countries has reduced, helped by the fact that transfer payments across borders have been part of the EU agenda to reduce inequality. However, inequality *within* countries has increased despite various regional aid packages. Within a country there is, of course, uniform monetary policy and the suggestion is that uniform monetary policy across members of a single currency (a necessity) will repeat the experience *within* countries and lead to greater inequality between these countries.

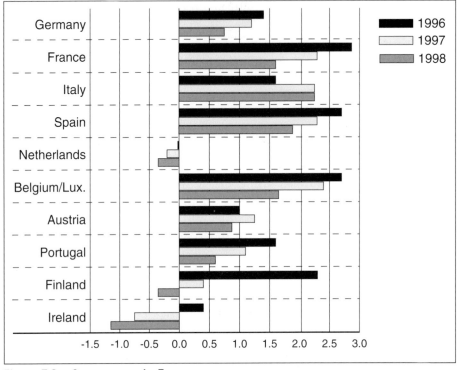

Figure 7.3   Output gaps in Europe

Source: *The Independent*, Tuesday 21 October 1997, article by Hamish McRae

All of this, of course, is unknown territory. The operation of the single currency may bring about changes in economic cycles, and regional inequalities may respond to more effective targeting with regional aid.

Pros and Cons of a Single Currency

Pros

1   Elimination of transactions costs – perhaps as much as ECU 20 billion (the cost of exchanging one EU currency into another is estimated by the European Commission as about 0.5 per cent of total EU GDP). Associated costs and delays will also be reduced.

2   Exchange rate uncertainty (not being sure what exchange rate will prevail when payment is made) or the need to take steps like hedging or futures purchase to eliminate uncertainty, will

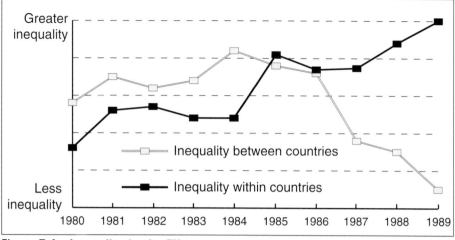

Figure 7.4   Inequality in the EU

Source: *The Independent, as above*

disappear for transactions between member currencies – but not, of course, for external currencies.

3   Distortion in cross-Union pricing should disappear as prices are expressed in the same currency. For example, variations in new car prices across the Union should become less common.

4   Greater price stability (low inflation) is likely as an independent European Central Bank pursues a low inflation agenda outside the influence of politicians. The Bundesbank in Germany has operated in this way over a long period, while one of the first acts of the newly-elected Labour government in Britain in 1997 was to similarly change the Bank of England.

5   A single market in financial services has tended to lag behind that in tangible goods. A single currency is likely to accelerate the single market in this area, as similar financial instruments (bonds, etc.) are expressed in one currency.

6   The status of the Single European Currency (comparable with the US dollar and the Japanese yen) will reduce the need for member states to hold reserves in external currencies. It will be advantageous to the EU that non-member countries hold higher reserves of the single currency.

Cons

1   The loss of autonomy in implementing economic policy is significant.

2   The European Central Bank which will control monetary policy is, as yet, untried. Its policies, despite its being the

servant of the Union, run the risk of either increasing demand too much to contain inflation, or restricting it too much to allow adequate economic growth.

What Business Thinks

For business, the issue of EMU is largely a pragmatic one. Studies carried out by the Confederation of British Industry show broad support. Accountants Coopers and Lybrand carried out a survey in 1996 of 1000 European companies with turnover in excess of £25 million. This set support for EMU in the UK at about 54 per cent for non-exporters and 65 per cent for exporters. This compared with a European average of 75 per cent for non-exporters and 85 per cent for exporters, with France and Italy topping 90 per cent.

Well-publicised pronouncements by multinational industrial leaders are made periodically to the effect that their company will have to consider its future investment in Britain if we do not join. The threat of these is both that Britain's continued membership of the EU might be threatened if we are outside the single currency, and also that the drawbacks of operating in a country retaining its domestic currency will be considerable.

Political

The deep divisions on Europe in general, and the single currency in particular, within the British Conservative Party in the run-up to the 1997 General Election was one of the dominant features of their campaign. Many observers consider that it played a significant role in the severity of their defeat. As the party of business (at least in the pre-Blair era), it was surprising to some that the Euro-sceptics were so dominant when the views of business and industry are generally pro-European and pro-EMU. It is, of course, the loss of sovereignty issue which sways many.

The post-election position of the Conservatives continued the theme. At the time of writing, a decision by the Shadow Cabinet to campaign against EMU at the next general election and thereby probably delay entry until at least 2007, should the Conservatives return to power, led to shadow cabinet resignations and no let-up in the internal conflict.

Labour's position prior to the election was less divided and generally pro-European. It was, however, distinctly lacking in clarity as to if and when a Labour government would take Britain into the Single European Currency. In the months after Labour's victory, things became more interesting but certainly no clearer. Leaks, briefings and articles provoked turmoil in both the City of Westminister. By early 1998, the Chancellor, Gordon Brown, had ruled out British entry to EMU before the next election. Beyond that, it is not known whether the Government will effectively put its weight behind the pro-lobby. It has been indicated that a referendum will be held on which our entry will depend.

The contrast between the political attitudes and positions in Britain and the rest of the European Union could hardly be more marked. Mainstream parties of both Left and Right in EU countries other than Britain support the principle and practice of EMU.

SIGNPOSTS TO ECONOMIC AND MONETARY INTEGRATION

1957	Treaty of Rome establishes the EEC
1962	Concept of economic and monetary union debate by the European Commission
1970	Werner Report advocated economic and monetary union
1979	European Monetary System (EMS) established. The Ecu is created
1986	Single European Act establishes the goal of free movement of goods, services, labour and capital, to be effected by 1 January 1993
1990	Britain joins ERM (October)
1991	Treaty on European Union (Maastricht) agreed. Firm commitment by member states to EMU by 1 January 1999 at the latest; 1997 favoured
1992	Britain and Spain 'temporarily' leave the ERM
1994	Stage Two of EMU. Establishment of European Monetary Institute (EMI). EMU draws up the necessary provisions for Stage Three
1995	Confirmation at Madrid Summit of Stage Three. agreement on 'Euro'
1997/1999	Stage Three of EMU. Conversion of those EC country currencies that meet convergence criteria to the Ecu. EMI becomes European Central Bank

---

'Delors 2' and the EC Cohesion Fund

The idea of the Cohesion Fund arose during the Maastricht Summit. The Fund, intended to be in operation by the end of 1993, would provide financial assistance for the poorer member states of the Union – Greece, Ireland, Portugal and Spain. The assistance would be granted for:

- the establishment within these states of appropriate parts of a trans-European energy, communications and transport network
- environmental improvement schemes

The political impetus behind the Fund proposal was the need to win backing from these poorer states for the goal of economic and monetary union by 1999. Only by offering some financial incentive could their support be assured.

The Fund was intended to be financed by the so-called 'Delors 2' package, suggested by the Commission President in early 1992. This would involve member states increasing their total financial contributions to the EC budget from the 1992 level of 66.5 billion Ecu to 86.2 billion Ecu by 1999.

The European Central Bank, European Monetary Institute and ECOFIN

The European Central Bank (ECB) grew out of the European Monetary Institute (EMI) which was established in 1994. On 1 June 1998 the ECB was established. The EMI is based in Frankfurt am Main in Germany. By the end of June 1998, the ECB had 450 members of staff mainly drawn from the central banks of the EU member states.

The Maastricht Treaty charged the EMI with tasks relating to Stages Two and Three of EMU (see box on page 171). The EMI did not have decision-making powers regarding monetary policy, but in the period up to 1999, when monetary policy remains in the hands of individual member states, it had a role in coordinating policies and promoting convergence.

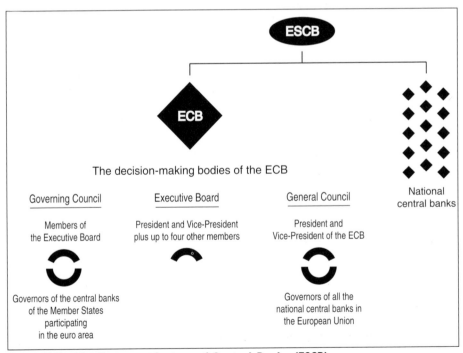

Figure 7.5   The European System of Central Banks (ESCB)
Source: The European Monetary Institute 97/European Central Bank 98

In preparation for Stage Three the EMI was required to 'specify the regulatory, organisational and logistical framework necessary for the European System of Central Banks (ESCB) to perform its tasks in the third stage'. The ESCB will have the following structure (see Figure 7.5):

Once the ECB begins to operate on 1 July 1999, also based in Frankfurt, member states' existing central banks will have to be independent of control by their respective governments, like the present German Bundesbank and, since 1997, the Bank of England. It is intended that the ECB will take the current German Bundesbank as its model; for example, one of its main policy objectives will be obtaining price stability throughout member states, as the Bundesbank does for Germany at present.

The ECB's Governing Council will be the ESCB's most important arm, as indicated by its membership (see Figure 7.5). It will make decisions on the ESCB's monetary policy. It is important to realise that this policy will only be implemented by member states which have adopted the Euro. The General Council will supplement the Governing Council for as long as there are members who have not adopted the single currency. This General Council will contain the Governors of all the Union's central banks to ensue they have a voice.

The European Parliament will receive annual reports from the ECB and will have the power to question the ECB President. It has the right to be both informed and consulted on aspects of EU monetary policy.

The European Council of Finance Ministers (ECOFIN) will, in consultation with the ECB, decide EU exchange rate policy. Once complete monetary union has been achieved, the European Commission will monitor member governments' budgets.

The ECB will, if it feels appropriate, via ECOFIN:

- issue warnings and/or recommend policy changes
- cut any credits that member states may be receiving from the European Investment Bank
- require member states to hand over a proportion of their non-interest-bearing deposits
- suspend EU regional aid
- impose fines

ECOFIN will also have the role of issuing broad economic guidelines in order to ensure that the European Union as a whole keeps to its stated economic objectives. If it feels that any individual member state is out of step and is following policies that it considers to be inconsistent with EMU, then it will have the power to issue 'recommendations' as to more appropriate policies.

Financial Services in the Single Market

Countries impose a number of restrictions on financial services activities across their borders, for a wide variety of reasons, including:

- to enable them to charge and collect tax
- to promote particular social and economic policies or other objectives

These restrictions have the effect of distorting to a greater or less degree the way in which financial markets operate. This in turn involves costs both to the individual and to the organisation.

The importance of financial services within the single market and the need for firms to have the right to obtain and trade in financial services freely throughout the EU, have grown over the last 15–20 years. Apart from the desire to allow market forces to operate in the provision of financial services, the pressure to extend the single market to financial services was further intensified by the growth and application of new technology in all the major financial centres of the world, thereby enabling cross-border transaction on a hugely expanded scale, thus intensifying global financial competition.

The Cecchini Report, referred to in Chapter 6, estimated that up to a third of the 4.5 per cent growth in Union GDP between 1992 and 1998 could be generated by the creation of a single market in financial services.

The Regulatory Background

EU Directive 85/611 set out the concept of a 'single authorisation passport' on 'Undertakings for Collective Investments in Transferable Securities' (UCITS). It states that once a UCITS has received the necessary approval in its home member country, it can be sold in other member states, subject to any regulations existing in those states with respect to, for example, marketing. This Directive is instrumental in assisting the EU to achieve its goal of the free movement of capital as laid down in the Treaty of Rome. The single market date was, of course, 1 January 1993 and member states were required to have passed relevant national legislation by that date. Home country authorisation, the issue of the 'passport', was to quickly follow.

In practice, the ability to trade financial services throughout the Union has been far from clear cut. Despite the above Directive, the second Banking Directive, which came into effect 1 January 1993, and the third Insurance Directive (Life and Non-Life) which came into effect 1 July 1994, barriers have hindered progress. Directives are often slow to be incorporated into member states' law; countries use domestic laws like Spain's 1994 limitation of the speed with which a new bank can open new branches, while tax differences between member states affect the operation of, for example, an insurance policy.

Two other directives are important: the Investment Services Directive and the Capital Adequacy Directive, both of which came into effect on 1 January 1996. The former also works on the 'passport' principle and, for instance, makes it even easier for a firm to sell securities in a country other than its home base. Rather than being required to set up a local subsidiary (as was required in Italy), a branch will be sufficient, or the transaction can be set up from the home base. The latter Directive sets common minimum capital requirements across the Union for banks and securities firms.

The European Commission published figures indicating that 10 countries would not have implemented the Capital Adequacy Directive by January 1996 and 8 countries would not have implemented the Investment Services Directive.

Developments in Banking and Insurance

In the late 1980s and early 1990s there was a trend towards bank mergers and an increased interest by these enlarged banks in areas of activity outside the traditional range of banking, in particular, insurance. The establishment of extensive pan-European financial groups seemed inevitable.

Events have not, however, moved as fast as might have been expected. Although the opening by banks of branches outside their base country increased by about 40 per cent in the two years following the establishment of the single market on 1 January 1993, banking remains more heavily based on domestic markets than other commercial areas. Companies like Aldi, Netto and McDonald's have become a common sight across borders. The most elaborate attempt at building a pan-European financial conglomerate was that of France's Credit Lyonnais which has run into severe problems. *The Economist* (14 October 1997) quotes a European insurance company as saying that 'most companies which have expanded overseas have lost money. It is essentially a strategy adopted by weak companies seeking to protect themselves'.

It is, of course, early days in terms of establishing a true single market in an area of commercial activity which is much more complex than that of groceries or fast food. Despite the Directives looked at above, member countries often retain, or have been slow to abandon, their own rules and regulations. For instance, the failure of Barclay's Bank to introduce interest-bearing current accounts in France was due to its prohibition by the Banque de France on the basis of its potential conflict with monetary policy. A further factor is that of customer loyalty – it is a lot less of an issue to switch one's shopping to a new supermarket, than to switch one's bank account to an unfamiliar newcomer.

There are, however, powerful reasons why the European financial sector is likely to become more integrated:

- The introduction of a single currency in the period from 1999 will simplify the administration of financial services across borders
- Very large financial institutions will only be able to expand by seeking wider markets abroad – their domestic market share can only be increased at disproportionate cost and effort. In insurance, where customer loyalty is less marked than in banking, integration is already more advanced and mergers give an easy way to enter a new market. Greater competition is, of course, the point of integration and an example of this is the reduction in German motor insurance premiums by the entry of insurance companies like France's AXA into the German market
- Modern financial services are heavily dependent on new technology. Investment in the latest technology is justified by large organisations and markets

Currency Transactions: Costs and Benefits

One of the consequences of European Monetary Union on the existing financial services sector, will be a sharp decline in the European market for 'futures'.

As a generalisation, contracts for the delivery of goods are of two types: 'spot' and 'forward'. In the case of 'spot', the person or organisation purchasing the goods will be expected to pay the contract price either when the goods are delivered or when the relevant contact papers are received., The 'spot' price is the market price prevailing at the time of agreement. Under 'forward' or 'futures' contracts, the contacted price does not have to be paid until an agreed specified date in the future. The goods in question may or may not have been delivered by that date.

'Forward' or 'future' prices are an agreed estimate as to what the prevailing 'spot' or market price will be at the time of delivery. This price is arrived at by taking into account such predictions as anticipated demand and supply conditions, rate of inflation etc.

The predicted 'future' market price may be higher or lower than that ruling at the time the original contact was made. If the spot price at the future date proves to be below the agreed price the seller would make a profit, if above the buyer would gain.

These transactions may be further complicated if the contract is to be paid for in foreign currency. Forward exchange rates apply, whereby a seller can agree a forward exchange rate that will be applied to the transaction in question. These rates are quoted by foreign exchange dealers. Forward exchange rates reduce the risks of sellers' income being unduly influenced by changes in market exchange rates.

At present, some 60 per cent of UK exports by value are with other European Union member states. The currency pressures of September 1992, resulting in the temporary withdrawal of the UK from the ERM, underline the need for those companies involved in importing and exporting within the EU to protect themselves from fluctuations in the value of the contract currency between the time of signing a contract and its completion. Economic and monetary union, with the planned introduction by January 1999 of a Single European Currency, the Euro, will remove this need and reduce the currency costs involved in intra-EU trade, currently estimated to be in the order of 7 billion to 12 billion Ecu.

The need for travellers between member states to convert currencies every time they cross a border will also be history by 1999 if EMU is achieved. There will thus be a benefit to the individual in terms of having more money to spend; but there will also be a loss to the financial services sector in terms of the profits currently made in commission on currency conversion.

The European Economic Area

In October 1991, agreement was reached between the EC and the European Free Trade Association (EFTA) to establish the EEA (European Economic Area). The EEA joined the EFTA countries (Austria, Finland, Iceland, Norway, Sweden, Switzerland) with the 12 EC countries, to form an enlarged common market population of 380 million. (Switzerland rejected EEA membership as a result of a referendum but retains EFTA membership.) This provided further impetus towards the establishment of a uniform and harmonised system for financial services as members of EFTA bring their existing financial services regulations into line with those that are being harmonised within the EU. Austria, Finland and Sweden joined the EU in 1995.

Direct Foreign Investment

Where capital funds move from one country to another, for

example, from Japan to the UK in order to set up a car factory in the UK, it is known as Direct Foreign Investment (DFI). DFI can be measured as either a flow over a period, or a stock. There has been rapid growth in the stock of DFI in recent years since both cost and marketing conditions can make this multinational activity worthwhile. For instance, Toyota or Nissan, both of whom set up car plants in the UK, would be attracted by our relatively low labour costs (compared to Germany, for example) and the fact that a plant here gives them access to the single market without the barriers they would face if simply exporting to the UK.

The growth of the stock of DFI ($US billion)

EU (Not including Austria, Sweden and Finland)

	1980	→	153
		←	143
	1990	→	477
		←	406
	1994	→	734
		←	524
US	1980	→	202
		←	83
	1990	→	435
		←	395
	1994	→	610
		←	504
Japan	1980	→	20
		←	3
	1990	→	201
		←	10
	1994	→	277
		←	18
South East Asia (excluding Japan)	1980	→	2
		←	32
	1990	→	38
		←	146
	1994	→	117
		←	305

Figure 7.6

Source: *Economics for Business,* Dermot McAlease, Prentice Hall, 1997

DFI into and from the EU, as well as on a worldwide basis, has increased sharply since 1980 (see Figure 7.6). This trend is likely to continue as part of an ongoing process of globalisation. Two questions are, however, of current interest:

- Will Britain's uncertainty about joining the single currency affect the flow of DFI into the country?
- Will the Labour Party's decision to embrace the Social Chapter make Britain a less attractive destination for DFI, particularly from countries like Japan?

Economic and Monetary Policy . . . What Next?

Students should monitor progress towards EMU and in particular the UK's position from 1999 until the General Election in 2002.

Other Internal Policies

This chapter covers:
★ The Common Agricultural Policy
★ Home Affairs, Justice and Immigration Policy
★ Employment, Social Affairs and Education Policy
★ Policies on the Environment, Health and Consumer Protection
★ Transport and Communication Policy
★ Energy Policy
★ Regional Policy
★ Industrial Policy

Introduction

The subjects of the previous two chapters on the single market and economic and monetary policy relate strongly to the original nature of the European *Economic* Community. However, as became clear in Chapter 3 on the European Treaties, since the Treaty of Rome was signed, the Union has become active in many more areas of life. This fundamental change in the nature of the Union was symbolised with the official change in its name from the European Economic Community (EEC), to the European Community (EC) in the Maastricht Treaty of 1991. The term 'European Union' was adopted in 1993 in recognition of the progress made towards the SEM and closer economic and political union.

This chapter sets out briefly the major provisions of European policy in seven important areas. It is not a comprehensive description of the entire range of the Union's activities, but will give you an idea of the scope of the Union's interests and powers in the affairs of its member states.

The Common Agricultural Policy

The Common Agricultural Policy (CAP) prevents prices of the main agricultural commodities, e.g. cereals, milk and lamb, being determined by the interaction of market forces, i.e. supply and demand.

Objectives

* To provide a minimum income for the European farming community
* To provide uniform agricultural prices throughout the EU
* To prevent one member state gaining competitive advantage over another due to the effect of agricultural prices on wage rates and unit costs of production
* To stabilise fluctuations in agricultural supplies and prices to consumers resulting from erratic annual harvests
* To raise agricultural productivity and release resources for other sectors of the economy

Mechanisms

* Maintenance of income for farmers via common external tariff, preventing inflow of cheap agricultural products from non-EU states
* Maintenance of income for farmers via official support (buying and selling) mechanisms, in order to maintain the current agricultural support price levels (intervention)

The CAP in Practice

Agriculture was one of the first industries to recover after the Second World War. Technology, both in terms of equipment and in terms of ways of improving the land, resulted in significant increases in production. However, increases in income for farmers did not follow automatically; agriculture, in large part because of its dependence on external factors such as weather, remains a notoriously volatile industry.

Despite being one of the most nearly completed common policies of the Union, the CAP has caused perhaps the greatest difficulties for member states of any policy area. Expenditure on CAP has taken a disproportionately large share of Union expenditure. Guaranteed prices which are far above world levels, including tariff protection against imports, have encouraged farmers to over produce. The so-called 'mountains' and 'lakes' of wheat, beef and wine have been purchased by the EU and either destroyed or sold unprofitably outside the EU. Efforts to reform the policy in such a way as to reduce this share have been fiercely resisted by those who benefit from its support. Conflict between member states with highly mechanised agricultural sectors and those with more traditional farming methods, has been a feature of the many attempts at CAP reform.

Many of the problems with beset the CAP in the early years of the Union, stemmed from fluctuations in exchange rates which should, in theory, be more stable in the ERM. As seen in Chapter 7, however, stability is not guaranteed. The long-standing Monetary Compensation Amounts (MCA) were levies and subsidies to compensate for currency-related distortions in agricultural trade within the EU. A turning point was the agreement in 1984 to base currency alignments on the Deutschmark, thereby tying prices to a stable currency. Not to do so, it was agreed, would bankrupt the Union. A Deutschmark rising against other currencies, however, led to unacceptable increases in agricultural prices. Milk quotas, also introduced in 1984, limited dairy production.

In 1992, Ray McSharry, the EU Farm Commissioner, carried out a number of reforms. The extremely controversial 'set aside' policy whereby farmers are paid *not* to produce from all their land was introduced. For the first time, the CAP's guaranteed cereal prices were cut and farmers were offered payments in compensation.

Despite general distaste for 'set aside' from farmers, agricultural businesses and environmentalists, the MacSharry reforms have had some success. The food 'mountains' have reduced and farm incomes have risen at a faster rate than before – in most countries of the Union they are above the national average wage. Cereal farmers have fared particularly well, benefiting both from the compensatory payments and increases in world prices (offsetting the CAP's price cuts).

The current Agriculture Commissioner, Franz Fischler, wishes to extend the MacSharry reforms. In the post-Amsterdam Summit period of late 1997, he proposed cuts in cereal, dairy and beef prices. Although compensation would be paid, the narrowing gap between EU and world prices would reduce the use of 'set aside'. Milk quotas would be continued until 2006. Despite the unpopularity of these reforms there appears to be some hope. Each country has its own interests to protect – for example, France, agriculturally the biggest EU producer, which has seen a halving of its farm population in 25 years, might accept lower prices in exchange for producing more, while Spain wishes to see its poor small farmers benefiting more at the expense of the rich North and so on. With the major slice of CAP subsidies traditionally going to a minority of rich farmers, the way forward may involve directing subsidies towards smaller farmers and allowing the level of compensatory payments to be at the discretion of member countries. Mr Fischler also wishes to link payments to farmers with environmental progress – an inevitably shrinking agricultural sector demands an imaginative handling of the whole rural economy.

The CAP will no doubt continue to be high on the agenda of the Union for many years to come.

Home Affairs, Justice and Immigration

Matters within these areas were considered at Maastricht and are set out in a supplementary protocol, not in the Treaty on European Union itself. The protocol sets out areas of common interest:

- Asylum policy
- Controls on external borders
- Immigration policy for nationals of non-EU states
- Combating drug addiction
- Combating fraud
- Judicial cooperation in civil matters
- Judicial cooperation in criminal matters
- Customs cooperation
- Police cooperation and the creation of Europol

The Treaty goes on to say that the areas of common interest identified shall be dealt with in compliance with the European Convention on Human Rights and Fundamental Freedoms. Member states agreed to consult one another with a view to coordinating action in these areas.

Employment, Social Affairs and Education

The Social Chapter of the Maastricht Treaty epitomised the widening and deepening of the Union's areas of concern to cover matters previously considered the preserve of individual countries. Indeed, at the Maastricht Summit in December 1991, the British government refused to accept the Social Chapter of the Treaty on the grounds that the matters contained within it were matters of national not Union competence. The other 11 member states, therefore, signed a protocol to adopt these articles which were not included in the Treaty itself. Those 11 member states confirmed their wish to implement the 1989 Social Chapter (see Chapter 2) and agreed the protocol on social policy as outlined below. (With the incoming Labour government of 1997, Britain's opt-out ended. However, Prime Minister Tony Blair has warned against burdensome labour-market regulation.)

Article 1

The Union and member states shall have as their objectives the promotion of employment, improved living and working conditions, proper social protection, dialogue between management and labour, the development of human resources with a view to lasting high employment and the combating of exclusion. To this end the Union and member states shall implement measures which take account of the diverse forms of national practices, in particular in the field of contractual relations and the need to maintain the competitiveness of the Union economy.

Article 2

Commits the Union to support member states in the following fields:

- working conditions
- the informing and consultation of workers
- equality of treatment between men and women
- the integration of persons excluded from the labour market

Progress in these areas is to be achieved by the implementation of Directives.

Additionally, operating unanimously, the Council of Ministers shall act in the following areas:

- social security and social protection of workers
- protection of workers when their employment contract is terminated
- representation and collective defence of the interests of workers and employers
- conditions of employment for non-Union nationals legally resident in a member state
- financial contribution for promotion of employment and job creation

The provisions of Article 2 do not apply to pay, the right of association, the right to strike of the right to impose lock-outs.

Article 3

Deals with the promotion of consultation between management and labour at Union level.

Article 4

Deals with the eventual promotion of contractual relations and agreements between management and labour.

Article 5

Encourages cooperation among member states and coordination of their action in all social policy fields.

Article 6

States that each member country shall ensure that the principle of equal pay for male and female workers for equal work is applied.

It also provides for appropriate positive measures to be taken to make it easier for women to pursue a vocational activity or to prevent or compensate for disadvantages in their professional careers.

Article 7

Provides for the Commission to draw up an annual report on progress to achieving the objectives set out in Article 1.

Works Councils

In 1994, the 11 signatories of the protocol voted to establish Works Councils in firms employing more than 1000 workers in the EU outside Britain. Because of Britain's opt-out, this included about 160 British companies because they employed more than 1000 people in the EU outside Britain and 150 employees in two or more of these countries. By mid-1996, 24 of these firms had Works Councils and a 1999 deadline was set for the establishment of the rest. However, interim arrangements required that if 100 or more employees requested it, a Special Negotiating Body (a sort of embryo Works Council) should be set up. With the end of Britain's opt-out from the Social chapter, more extensive implementation of Works Councils will take place, but not before the end of 1999.

The European Citizen

The Maastricht Treaty set out for the first time the rights in respect of the Union possessed by every individual who is a national of a member state. Article 8 of the Treaty:

- creates citizenship of the European Union and gives it to every person holding the nationality of a member state
- gives free movement for citizens without the Union, subject to the existing conditions in the Treaty of Rome
- gives each citizen the right to stand and vote in municipal elections in the member state in which he or she resides
- gives the citizen the right to stand and vote in elections for the European Parliament in the member state in which he or she resides
- gives the citizen the protection of diplomatic authorities of any member state when he or she is in a third country where his or her own does not have representation
- gives the right to petition the European Parliament and use the European Ombudsman

Education, Vocational Training and Youth Matters

Articles 126 and 127 of the Maastricht Treaty set out the following principles.

1 The Union shall contribute to the development of quality

education by encouraging cooperation between member states whilst respecting their rights to organise their own education systems. In particular, the Union shall aim to:
- develop the European dimension in education
- encourage mobility of teachers and students, especially by the mutual recognition of diplomas and periods of study
- develop exchanges of information and experience
- encourage exchanges of young people and socio-educational instructors
- encourage the development of distance learning

2 The Union shall implement a vocational training policy. Union action shall aim to:
- facilitate industrial changes through vocational training and retraining
- improve vocational training in order to facilitate vocational integration and reintegration into the labour market
- facilitate access to vocational training and encourage mobility
- stimulate cooperation on training between educational or training establishments and firms
- develop exchanges of information and experience

The Union and member states shall foster cooperation with third countries and competent international organisations in the sphere of vocational training.

Culture

Article 128 of the Maastricht Treaty states that:

The Community shall contribute to the flowering of the cultures of the member states while respecting their national and regional diversity and at the same time bringing the common cultural heritage to the fore.

Action by the Union shall be aimed at encouraging cooperation between member states and, if necessary, supporting and supplementing their actions in the following areas:

- improvement of the knowledge and dissemination of the culture and history of the European peoples

- conservation and safeguarding of cultural heritage of European significance

- non-commercial cultural exchanges

- artistic and literary creation, including the audio-visual sector

The Environment, Health and Consumer Protection

Protecting the Environment

Article 130 of the Maastricht Treaty identifies the following central objectives in the community policy on the environment:

- Preserving, protecting and improving the quality of the environment
- Protecting human health
- Prudent and rational utilisation of natural resources
- Promoting international measures to deal with environmental problems

The policy is based on the principle that preventative action should be taken, that environmental damage should be rectified at source and that the polluter should pay. Member states are not prevented from introducing measures more stringent than those of the Union, so long as these are notified to the Commission and are not incompatible with the Treaty.

Public Health

Article 129 of the Maastricht Treaty states that the Union 'shall contribute towards ensuring a high level of human health protection by encouraging cooperation between member states and, if necessary, lending support to their actions. Union action shall be directed towards the prevention of diseases, in particular the major health scourges, including drug dependence, by promoting research into their causes and their transmission, as well as health information and education'.

Article 129 also provides for the harmonisation of laws, the introduction of regulations and the adoption of incentives to contribute to the achievement of these aims. The provisions of the Treaty, therefore, envisage greater cooperation among member states to prevent drug addition and the spread of Aids.

The Council of Ministers will be able to adopt recommendations in the public health field by qualified majority voting, and member states will, under the Treaty, coordinate their public health programmes and policies with the European Commission.

Consumer Protection

Article 127A of the Maastricht Treaty states that:

1   The Union shall contribute to a high level of consumer protection through measures adopted through Article 100A.

Article 100A relates to the adoption by qualified majority voting of measures to harmonise national law in order to complete the internal market.

2   The Union shall take specific action in addition to that undertaken in member states to protect the health, safety and economic interest of consumers and to provide them with adequate information.

3   Member sates may introduce more stringent measures as long as they are not incompatible with the Treaty and the Commission is informed.

Transport and Communications

The original Treaty of Rome contained numerous provisions about the creation of a common European transport policy. Harmonisation of transport was seen as a cornerstone of the creation of an energetic and prosperous internal market.

However, transport policy failed to be implemented holistically by member states in the early years of the Community, and was allowed to develop only patchily; protectionist practice remained (and still remains) in this area of community activity.

The main provisions of Union policy on transport are contained in Articles 74–84 of the Treaty of Rome. The terms in which the Treaty sets out the transport policy are noticeable more vague than the terms in which other policies are set out.

Article 75

The Council shall ... by a qualified majority lay down ...

a)   common rules applicable to international transport to or from the territory of a member state ...

b)   the conditions under which non-resident carriers may operate transport services within a member state.

Article 76

Prohibits discrimination by member states against carriers of other member states.

Article 77

Enables states, however, to subsidise transport as a public service or for the purposes of coordination.

Deregulation of transport and the creation of an internal market in transport services was seen by the Commission as one of the key factors in the establishment of free movement of goods across the

Union. From 1 January 1993, road hauliers (previously one of the groups which suffered most from the costs of non-Europe) have had complete freedom to carry out international journeys within the Union.

Agreement on the problem of cabotage, a system which allows a haulier to pick up goods in member states other than his own and transport them within that member state, was reached in June 1993 as an offshoot of an agreement on a common system of charging trucks for using EC roads. Until this agreement, scarce licences were necessary to practice cabotage – these covered less than 1 per cent of the market in such haulage. The level of 18,530 licences would be raised to 30,000 in January 1994 and then by 30 per cent annually, leading to full cabotage by 1 July 1998.

A stumbling block to cabotage was how to charge hauliers for road use (necessary to level out transport costs and minimise unfair competitive advantage under cabotage) with Germany refusing to open its roads to outside competition in the absence of common charging. Eventual agreement was reached by Germany, Holland, Belgium, Luxembourg and Denmark on an annual fee of ECU 1250 and display of a disc. Road charging was agreed in principle by most of the then 12 members, including Britain.

In air transport, cross-border restrictions on prices and schedules disappeared in 1993, but prices remain high with few new carriers and state-aided national carriers making entry to the markets difficult. A single system of air traffic control, identified by Transport Commissioner Neil Kinnock as highly desirable, remains a long way off.

Trans-European Networks

The Maastricht Treaty introduced the concept of trans-European networks in the areas of transport, telecommunications and energy infrastructure, in order to enable citizens of the European Union, economic operators and regional and local communities to derive the full benefit from the setting-up of an area without internal frontiers.

It stated that the Union should contribute towards the establishment of these networks, aiming to promote the interconnection and interoperability of national networks, as well as access to common European networks. It also noted that particular account needed to be taken of the need to link remote regions with the central regions of the Union.

A list of 14 such projects was approved by the EU in 1994, costing ECU 90 billion. The EU's most ambitious transport project dates from 1995. By 2010, it aims to have created a ECU 300 billion transport network to link peripheral countries with the centre of Europe. This would benefit countries with poor transport systems, such as Greece. TENS (trans-European networks) have proved difficult to implement and form part of Transport Commissioner Kinnock's agenda. Job creation on a large scale is one of their attractions, but funding is a stumbling block – the EU has provided start-up funds, but as public expenditure is reigned-in during the run-up to EMU, countries are hesitant to provide the balance. As recently as September 1996, the European Parliament's President was berating EU states for withholding ECU one billion for TENS.

Energy

The coordination and development of safe energy policies was an important element of the philosophy behind the establishment of the EEC in the 1950s. The Schuman Plan, adopted by the original six signatories to the Treaty of Rome, was designed to create a common market for coal and steel and was signed by the six in Paris on 18 April 1951. It prohibited import and export duties on these products and measures having equivalent effect, as well as outlawing discriminatory and restrictive practices in the coal and steel industries.

At the same time as the Treaty of Rome establishing the European Economic Community was signed on 25 March 1957, a second treaty was signed which provided for the establishment of the European Atomic Energy Community, or EURATOM. This instruction was set up in order to ensure the peaceful development of nuclear energy on a pan-European basis. The UK (not a signatory) had a well-developed atomic energy capability and the six signatories to EURATOM saw their cooperation as a way of ensuring that they kept up with the UK from both the technological and the safety point of view.

The Brussels Treaty of 1965 (otherwise known as the Merger Treaty), had the effect of combining the Economic, Coal and Steel, and Atomic Energy Communities into the same institutional framework.

In recent years, the common energy policies of the Union have faded from the spotlight as more emphasis has come to be placed on the development of economic policies and the establishment of the Single European Market. However, the Maastricht Treaty provides for the establishment of trans-European networks (see page 189) and envisages that technological and other barriers shall be dismantled in order to ensure the development of networks in the areas of transport, telecommunications and energy.

The Treaty envisages that the Cohesion Fund (which exists to boost the economies of poorer or remoter areas of the Community) could be used to finance the establishment of such networks by the provision of loans, guarantees and feasibility studies.

The Maastricht Treaty provides for new policies to be laid down in the field of energy, but made no detailed provisions. A report by the European Environment Agency in 1995, concluded that the EU's policies are inadequate to address the effects on health of low energy price and insufficient improvements in energy efficiency.

Regional Policy

The European Union is very diverse, both between and within member countries. Regional aid has been available during the history of the Union, but as a result of factors like increasing urbanisation and new members joining, a new set of structural funds was established in 1994. Objective Areas for the purposes of Regional Policy are defined as follows:

THE OBJECTIVES OF STRUCTURAL FUND ACTION

Objective 1: promoting the development and structural adjustment of regions whose development is lagging behind.

Objective 2: converting the regions seriously affected by industrial decline.

Objective 3: combating long-term unemployment and facilitating the integration into working life of young people and of people exposed to exclusion from the labour market; promoting equal opportunities for men and women in the labour market.

Objective 4: facilitating the adaptation of workers to industrial change and to changes in production systems.

Objective 5: promoting rural development by:

- speeding up the adjustment of agricultural structures in the framework of the reform of the Common Agricultural Policy
- facilitating the development and structural adjustment of rural areas.

Objective 6: promoting the development and structural adjustment of regions with an extremely low population density.

Source: *Sources of European Community Funding,* European Commission

---

About 80 per cent of Structural Funds go to Objective 1. Structural Funds are allocated under three headings:

The European Regional Development Fund (ERDF)

Regions bid for money under the ERDF on the basis that funds received are *additional* to those available nationally and they are therefore spent on additional projects. Most ERDF funds would come under Objectives 1 and 2. Regions eligible under Objective 1 in Britain are Northern Ireland, Merseyside and The Highlands and Islands of Scotland.

The European Social Fund (ESF)

The ESF is concerned primarily with encouraging job creation in areas of high unemployment. To this end, training and retraining support the acquisition of new skills.

The European Agricultural Guidance and Guarantee Fund

This is the mechanism for delivering the funds dealt with earlier in the section on the Common Agricultural Policy.

Reform of the Structural Funds is due to be completed by 1999. The Social Affairs Commissioner, Padraig Flynn, and the Structural Instruments Commissioner, Monika Wulf-Mathies, have called for a radical simplification, with member states having a bigger role in the implementation of the Funds. These amounted to ECU 38 billion in 1997. It has been suggested that the Objective Areas listed above should be simplified into two:

- The economic and social development of the poorer or industrially declining regions
- The development on an EU-wide basis of human resources, to include training and education

The need for funds to be additional to those available nationally is being examined. It may sometimes be desirable for funds to be spent on existing projects – the danger, and the reason for the additionality rule in the first place, is that EU funds sometimes replace domestic funds.

Industrial Policy

The Treaty of Rome did not contain a plan for a formal industrial policy in the way that agriculture, for example, was covered. However, areas such as competition (directly relevant to industrial policy) were covered, and Article 2 talked of:

progressively approximating the economic policies of member states, to promote throughout the Community a harmonious development of economic activities, a continuous and balanced expansion ... and closer relations between the states belonging to it.

The Maastricht Treaty talked of ensuring the existence of conditions necessary for the competitiveness of the EU's industry, adjustment to structural change and encouragement of research and development. Specific measures were provided for in order to promote this. The Industrial Policy currently has four priority areas, which are as follows:

1   Promotion of intangible investments, e.g. intellectual property, with legislation being strengthened and research more closely linked to needs.

2   Development of industrial cooperation. Given that a major reason for having an industrial policy is to secure EU competitiveness against other countries, this involves both links between EU and non-EU companies and global implications for market-dominating EU companies.

3   Ensuring fair competition and negotiating World Trade Organisation (the successor to GATT) provisions.

4   To improve Single European Market operation and modernise the way public authorities function.

Other Internal Policies ... What Next?

Students should:

–   Monitor Britain's adoption of the Social Chapter in such areas as Works Councils and Minimum Wage.
–   Trace reforms in the CAP in the years up to and immediately following the Millennium.

The EU and the Wider World

This chapter covers:

★ The Common Foreign and Security Policy
★ The EU and GATT
★ The World Trade Organisation
★ EU relations with the USA and Japan
★ The EU and world trade
★ The EU and Eastern Europe
★ The EU and developing countries

Introduction: Fortress Europe?

The idea which is sometimes touted of Europe as a 'rich man's club' is one which no longer holds good when examined alongside the EU's growing influence within the world. The view of the EU as a cartel of rich, developed countries, whose members jealously guard their own interests and whose energies are devoted to helping each other whilst turning their collective back on the rest of the world, is known as the 'Fortress Europe' syndrome. This is a criticism previously levelled by other Superpowers, particularly business interests in the USA. This chapter illustrates just how committed the EU is to working with countries from all corners of the globe. It examines the EU's relationships with the world outside its boundaries from two perspectives:

- Firstly, that of foreign and security policy – how the EU can forge a shared approach to matters affecting its standing in the world and the security of its member states.
- Secondly, that of trade and aid relations – how the EU relates to other players and organisations in the world economy: GATT, the USA and Japan, trading blocks such as NAFTA and ASEAN, and to other groups of countries, specifically the countries of Eastern Europe and those of the developing world.

It is worth noting that the EU accounts for over a fifth of world trade in goods and 10–12 million jobs depend on it – reason enough for abandoning the concept of Fortress Europe.

The Common Foreign and Security Policy

Chapter J of the Maastricht Treaty states: 'A common foreign and security policy is hereby established.' The objectives of such a policy are identified as follows:

- To safeguard the common values, fundamental interests and independence of the Union
- To strengthen the security of the Union and its member states in all ways
- To preserve peace and strengthen international security
- To promote international cooperation
- To develop and consolidate democracy and the role of law, and respect for human rights and fundamental freedom

The EU's common foreign and security policy is intended to operate in a different way from other Union policies, as a result of compromises which were made at the Maastricht summit. In a federal state such as the USA or Germany, foreign and security policies are a matter for the federal authorities, not for the individual state (in the USA) or *Land* (in Germany). This is not the situation with the European Union, even though the Maastricht Treaty states that when it is ratified, a common foreign and security policy is thereby created.

If the common foreign and security policy had been made a policy of the Union in the same way as, for example, competition policy, that would mean that member states would be subjecting themselves in this important area to the supervision of the institution of the Union, notably the European Court of Justice. This would be a radical step for the member states to take. The ability of a national state to determine its own foreign and security policy is an important measure of its sovereign status. For example, countries 'recognise' new states – on independence, or after revolutions or divisions, as in the recognition of the countries which have emerged from the former Yugoslavia. In this recognition lies the assumption that as a sovereign state, a country can 'confer' sovereign status on another country.

Any question, therefore, of surrendering (or even pooling) sovereignty in this area to an EU institution was likely to be resisted very strongly. Therefore, although the Maastricht Treaty contains provisions which establish a common foreign and security policy, it is important to understand that in practice what was agreed at Maastricht was a compromise between national traditions and sensitivities on the one hand, and the 'European ideal' on the other.

According to the agreement that was reached at Maastricht, the European Council may agree joint EU action in a particular foreign-policy area. The Treaty does not imply that *all* foreign policy should be decided. Once a particular policy stance has been agreed, then the policy will be implemented jointly and without an individual member state being able to veto the implementation. Which matters come within the scope of the joint action is for the Council to decide.

In a case of what the Treaty calls an 'imperative need', where the situation has changed and the Council has not acted, member states may take necessary measures as a matter of urgency and inform the Council immediately.

The Common Defence Policy

The formulation of a common EU defence policy is complicated not only by the membership of certain of the member states in NATO, but also by the existence of the defence-oriented organisation the Western European Union, which includes nine of the 15 EU member states.

In view of these existing obligations, the Maastricht Treaty arrived at the following statements:

- The common foreign and security policy shall include all questions related to the security of the Union, including the eventual framing of a common defence policy which might in time lead to a common defence (Article J4)
- The policy of the WEU shall respect NATO obligations and not prejudice national policies in this area
- The WEU shall have a strengthened role in the defence component of the Union
- Member states not in the WEU shall be invited to join

For the latest developments, refer to Chapter 3.

The EU and GATT

GATT (the General Agreement on Tariffs and Trade) was founded after the Second World War (1947) with the objective of opening up and freeing world trade in order to boost the world economy. By 1995, it had almost 130 members. GATT works on the principle of eliminating protective trade barriers and making multilateral agreements amongst member states which do not discriminate against any of its members. It also functions as a negotiating body should any trade disputes or problems occur amongst its members, and helps to establish rules for the conduct of world trade.

The European Commission negotiates with GATT to represent the 15 member states. GATT holds rounds of talks which culminate every few years in an agreement on specific categories of goods. Not surprisingly with over 130 members, the later rounds of talks have proved lengthy and at times unwieldy and have taken several years to complete. There have been a number of rounds to date, the most famous of which are the Kennedy, Nixon, Tokyo and most recently the Uruguay round.

The Uruguay round has been rather controversial. Started in 1986, it aimed amongst other things to extend GATT policies to agricultural products. This immediately sparked a conflict between the EU and the US representatives. The USA objected to the large subsidies enjoyed by European farmers, suggesting that these represented an unfair advantage in world trade over US farmers. Negotiations over the subsidies staggered on over several years, only to founder spectacularly in 1992.

Internal wranglings and disagreements amongst EU members adversely affected the Union's ability to negotiate effectively. The USA, tiring of the delay in reaching an agreement, seized the initiative and forced the EU to conclude the negotiations or face the threat of a trade war. A tentative agreement was reached at the end of 1992, but the episode inevitably soured US–EU relations, reviving the accusations of 'Fortress Europe'. Suggestions that the EU is prepared to deal with external trading nations only on its own terms, must inevitably harm the global trading environment.

As a worldwide organisation, GATT has to take into account all of its members' wishes, but it is perhaps inevitable that major players like the USA and the EU figure prominently in its negotiations.

The Uruguay round also considered the services sector and looked to provide protection for intellectual property (particularly in relation to counterfeit or pirated goods). Despite the arduous negotiations, the round was concluded satisfactorily in December 1993, providing a projected boost of approximately ECU 130 billion to world trade by 2005, which was a credit to all of the participants.

World Trade Organisation

Established in 1995, the World Trade Organisation (WTO)

supercedes and builds on the earlier role of GATT. Its membership of over 150 countries works towards five major objectives:

- To administer multilateral trade arrangements
- To facilitate further trade negotiations
- To settle disputes
- To oversee national trade policies
- To act as coordinator/negotiator with other international bodies on global economic matters and strategies

The WTO's purpose is to oversee and operate a set of rules which allow free, open and fair trade. It has a wider remit than GATT and covers trade in goods, services, ideas and intellectual property. It has an annual budget of approximately 80 million US dollars and is a permanent institution.

The EU, the USA and Japan

Global trading means that even powerful economics have to remain aware of the effect economies can have upon each other. The cliché of the USA sneezing and Europe catching a cold is truer than ever. Whilst trading blocs and erstwhile superpowers are busy marshalling their own forces, it is inevitable that their economies are interdependent to some degree. The economic crises in the Far East in late 1997, rattled most of the Western European nations. The frailty of the previously strong 'tiger' economies impacted both jobs and investment in the UK and other European nations.

From the viewpoint of the USA, the European single market programme can be viewed both as an opportunity and as a threat. For many multinational companies (whether American or Japanese) that have already established a base in Europe, the EU internal market represents a major business opportunity for the 1990s and beyond. Other companies, particularly medium-sized enterprises, may see it as a threat. It may become tougher for such companies to export into the EU should the external frontiers become more difficult to penetrate. As the EU has enjoyed a trading surplus with the USA in recent years, it would appear that the Union holds many aces.

The European Union and World Trade

Figure 9.1 shows just how significant a player the European Union has become in world-trade terms.

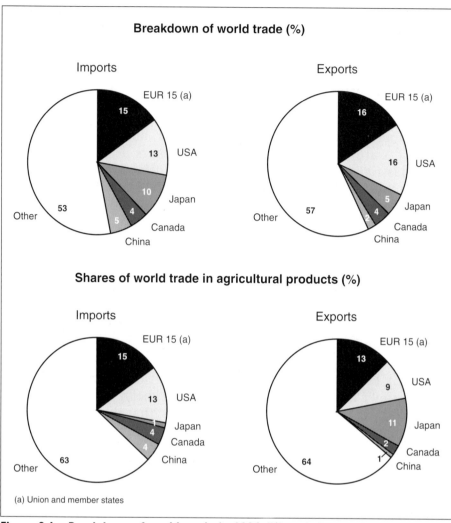

Figure 9.1 **Breakdown of world trade in 1994 (%) and shares of world trade in agricultural products in 1994 (%)**

Source: *External Trade Monthly,* Eurostat

Whilst they may be trading rivals, the EU and the USA are allies sharing certain values. In 1990, the USA and the member states of the EU signed the Transatlantic Declaration which gave political support to the continuation of a stable, democratic European partner. The Triad, as it is known (EU, US and Japan), continues to be a dominant force in global economics.

The EU, EFTA and the EEA

The European Free Trade Association was founded in 1960 by Austria, Denmark, Norway, Portugal, Sweden, Switzerland and the UK as a response to the then fledgling EEC. It was, as its name indicates, primarily a free-trade association and initially the UK hoped that the EEC would seek membership of EFTA. This would enable the UK and EEC members to trade freely without harming the trade of the Commonwealth countries whose interests the UK was hoping to preserve. This proposal was unlikely to succeed, and by 1961 the UK had decided that its future lay with that of the EEC and had made its first application for membership. EFTA continued, however, and today the EU and EFTA are very important trading partners. EFTA comprises four industrialised and wealthy countries: Iceland, Liechtenstein, Norway and Switzerland. A number of these countries could undoubtedly contribute to the EU if they were member states, and all have already applied for EU membership, although both Norway and Switzerland's citizens have voted against joining in referenda.

The close relationship between the EU and EFTA culminated in the creation in 1991 of the EEA (European Economic Area). This agreement created a trading bloc of 19 countries (12 EU states plus the seven EFTA members) and allowed the EFTA countries to join the single market programme on 1 January 1993, enjoying the benefits of free movement of goods, services, capital and labour. EFTA also pledged to follow EU legislation on company and consumer law, as well as education and social policy. It has been said by certain political commentators, that the EEA acts as an antechamber for countries wishing to become full members of the EU. For example, Sweden, Finland and Austria were all members of the EEA before they joined the EU in 1995.

As these three prior members of the EEA – Sweden, Finland and Austria – joined the EU in 1995, the focus of the EEA has become rather unclear. It is possible that it will continue to function for countries wanting to be economically integrated with the EU, but who are not yet ready to become politically integrated.

The European Union and Eastern Europe

Following the 1989 revolutions, Europe appears to be a much more stable continent with many of the newly democratised countries joining the free-market scramble and casting envious glances at the relatively prosperous economies of the EU member states.

The requirements for membership of the Union are quite specific. The candidate has to be European and democratic in nature. One of the major stumbling blocks is that a prospective candidate is expected to be able to integrate fully into the economic activities of the Union (following a short transitional period) and this obviously has acted as a brake on expansion.

Whilst the manoeuvering and posturing takes place within the existing member states pre-EMU, it is unlikely that new member states will be welcomed by the year 2000, although some countries eager to join were hoping that negotiations might start in 1998. The earliest date for admission currently being touted is 2002 and that might yet be pushed back even further. A major attraction of membership is the ability to anchor the independence and sovereignty of the new democracies. In economic terms, many of these newly enfranchised states already trade heavily with the EU and share many of the benefits of the Single European Market under their Europe agreements. The Union itself needs to look to the reform of some of its key policies (most notably the CAP and its regional policies) before offering full membership to the current list of applicants.

Alternatively, because of the problems they themselves are experiencing trying to meet the convergence criteria of Maastricht, the existing members could suggest a very long transitional period to applicants before full membership is granted, in order to iron out economic problems. Two major problem areas exist: that of the former Yugoslavia and the former USSR. The tenuous peace process in the former Yugoslavia will determine its relationship with the EU, so the future is somewhat unclear. This is also the case with Russia and members of the Commonwealth of Independent States. The Partnership Agreements concluded in June 1994 between the EU, Russia and the Ukraine aim to establish a free-trade area by the year 2000, in addition to developing their market economies and stabilising their currencies.

Full integration within the EU is a big step. In June 1993, the Copenhagen European Council confirmed that associated countries in central and eastern Europe could accede to the EU.

> Accession will take place as soon as an associated country is able to assume the obligations of membership by satisfying the economic and political conditions required.

The list of conditions is fairly demanding:

- Stable democratic institutions
- Respect for minorities
- The existence of a market economy able to withstand competitive pressure within the EU
- The ability to adhere to the aims of political, economic and monetary union

Enlargement must come in the new millennium, but at the time deemed right by the current 15 member states.

The EU and Developing Countries

It has always been one of the EU's objectives to promote links with the worldwide community. Article 110 of the Treaty of Rome contains the commitment in principle to:

> Contribute, in the common interest, to the harmonious development of world trade, the progressive abolition of restrictions in international trade and the lowering of customs barriers.

The European Development Fund created in 1958 was set up for this purpose, followed in 1963 by the Yaounde Convention.

TRADE, AID AND COOPERATION AGREEMENTS

1958	European Development Fund created
	Purpose: To work for the fulfilment of Article 100 of the Treaty of Rome
1963	Yaounde Convention signed, including 18 African countries and Madagascar
	Purpose: To provide aid to the African region
1975	First Lomé Convention signed, including 69 African, Caribbean and Pacific countries
	Purpose: To give help in emergencies and to foster long-term development
1979	Second Lomé Convention
1984	Third Lomé Convention
1989	Fourth Lomé Convention

The following statistics give an idea of how committed the EU is to the Developing World.

- The EU absorbs 22 per cent of Third World exports
- In 1991, development aid to the Third World came to 3.8 billion US dollars or 5.7 per cent of total Community expenditure
- Aid from the Community increased by 35 per cent between 1988 and 1991

Humanitarian Aid

The EU is not only active in giving economic aid to developing countries. Its humanitarian aid includes emergency and, in the case of national disasters or conflicts, long-term aid and food aid for refugees and the vulnerable. It is given irrespective of economic system or political tendency.

The Lomé Conventions

The first Lomé Convention was signed in 1975 by the EU and 46 African, Caribbean and Pacific (ACP) countries. The fourth, in 1989, was signed by the then 12 member states and 69 ACP countries. Many of these countries have close links with member states, particularly those which are ex-colonies.

The Lomé Convention is the largest single aid programme in the world and is negotiated and updated at regular intervals. It aims to give help in emergencies but simultaneously to work towards long-term development. Its objectives, to be achieved through a process of negotiation are:

- To promote rural development and combat hunger
- To strengthen partners' economics and lessen dependence
- To gain lasting improvements to peoples' living standards

Lomé IV is intended to cover the 10-year period from 1990 to 2000. It has three main elements: trade, aid and cooperation. The EU is to give 12 billion ECU's-worth of aid in the form of loans and grants over the first five years. This aid is non-repayable, apart from risk capital and loans from the European Investment Bank. Lomé also grants preferential access to EU markets for ACP products; such access to the worlds' richest markets should provide a boost to each ACP country's economy. There are also benefits for the EU under this system: EU exports into ACP countries enjoy 'most favoured nation' (MFN) status, which gives them preferential access to ACP markets.

The Lomé programme is one which allows the developing countries considerable self-direction. It is a politically neutral programme which promotes cooperation between governments of differing political opinions. It works on the principle of allowing the ACP countries a great degree of self-determination in the allocation of aid. Power is shared between the EU and the ACP countries, with joint decision making on particular projects. The whole system is underwritten by a continuous dialogue between the EU and ACP governments and institutions, allowing for cooperation and progress.

Latin America

Links between the EU and Latin America have multiplied and strengthened dramatically over the last two decades. The first wave of cooperation agreements between the EU and Latin America were made in the 1970s with Brazil and Uruguay, and concerned trade alone. The third-generation agreements of the 1990s encompass the whole mainland, and cover a much wider range of

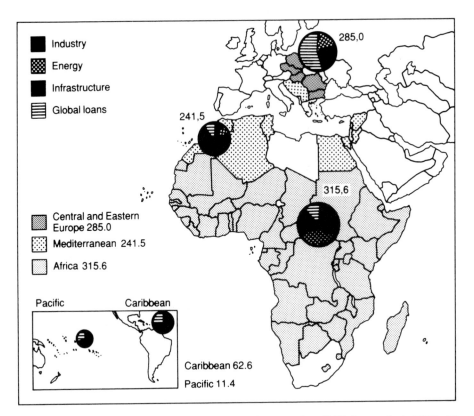

Figure 9.2 Financing provided outside the Community (ACP Countries) 1993–97 (million Ecus)

Source: European Investment Bank

topics, some of which are particularly pertinent to that continent. In addition to trade, the environment and the containment of the drugs problem, there is also provision for economic, industrial, scientific and technical cooperation. The region has also been the recipient of food and humanitarian aid.

Latin America is a key future market for the EU, accounting for 20 per cent of both the EU's imports and exports. This has resulted in Latin America using the Generalised System of Preferences for its trade, which grants it easier access to European markets for its products. This system also aims to encourage and support the exporting policies of the exporting countries. Its use should foster the development of the existing promising situation into an excellent and thriving long-term trading relationship.

Asia

Agreements broadly similar to those made with Latin American countries have been made between the EU and several Asian

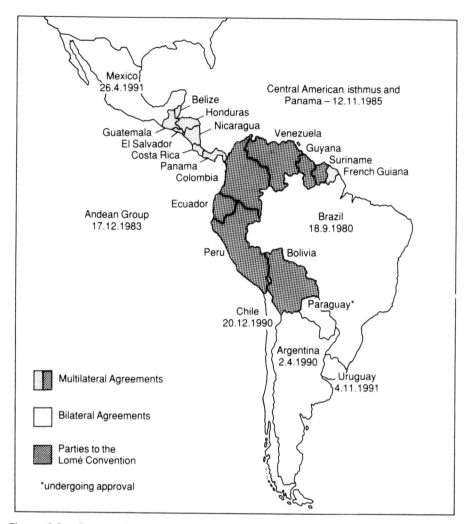

Figure 9.3 Cooperation agreements with the countries of Latin America (each partner's name is followed by the date on which the relevant agreement was signed)

countries. Asian countries are entitled to preferential treatment under the EU's Generalised System of Preferences for exports from developing countries, and to financial aid from the EU budget.

A regional agreement was made in 1980 with ASEAN (Association of South East Asian Nations) whose members today comprise Brunei, Indonesia, Malaysia, the Philippines, Singapore and Thailand. This established a framework for business, economic and development cooperation. The framework allows for continuous dialogue, with particular emphasis on the promotion of European investment in the region.

Mediterranean Countries

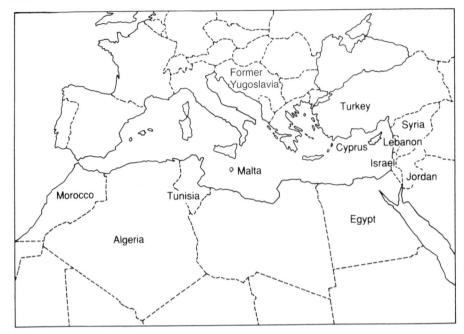

Figure 9.4   Mediterranean countries that have concluded agreements with the Community

The countries bordering the Mediterranean Sea have a natural trading link with the EU because of their proximity and shared history. It is also vital to the EU that this area remains stable, both economically and politically, so it is very much in the interests of the EU to promote sound links which foster prosperity within this region. The 1960s saw the first limited agreements, and by 1975 cooperation agreements had been concluded with Morocco, Algeria, Tunisia, Egypt, Jordan, Syria and the Lebanon.

The EU and the Mediterranean countries have much to gain from an interdependent relationship. The EU exports 30 billion US dollar's-worth of goods and services into the Mediterranean and receives goods worth 25 billion US dollars back. This makes the Mediterranean a more significant trading partner than Japan. Most Mediterranean countries depend heavily on exporting to the EU. There is also a large-scale movement into the EU from these countries of people seeking work.

The EU wishes to encourage the Mediterranean countries to become more self-reliant in terms of development. Towards this end, the Union implemented the New Mediterranean Policy in 1990. This Policy aims to support and encourage the Mediterranean countries in moves towards a freer economic system and a more democratic political system. The Policy was being put to the test in 1993 in war-torn Yugoslavia, where the EU have endeavoured to help in many ways. The Policy was supported by an aid package of ECU 4,405 million.

FACTFILE ON THE EU'S AID PROGRAMME

- 107 Third World countries have cooperation agreements with the EU
- In 1998, EC development aid amounted to US$2.9 billion, which accounts for 5.4 per cent of EU expenditure
- Aid from the EU and the individual member states accounts for 36 per cent of world aid

---

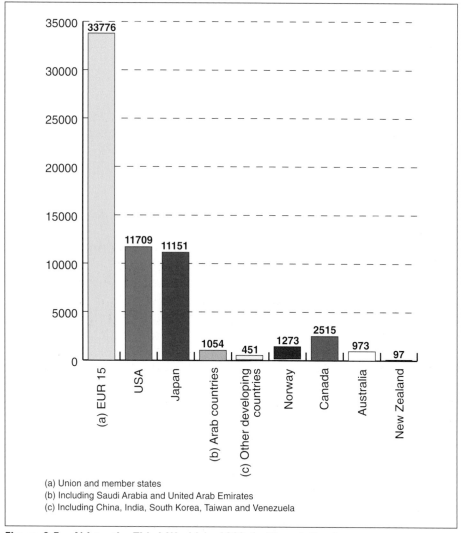

(a) Union and member states
(b) Including Saudi Arabia and United Arab Emirates
(c) Including China, India, South Korea, Taiwan and Venezuela

Figure 9.5   Aid to the Third World in 1992 (million dollars)

Source: Eurostat

The EU and the Wider World ... What Next?

Students may wish to consider the following:

–   How may the EU further develop links with the Developing
    World?

–   To what extent does world trade benefit from trading blocs?

10 *The European Union into the Twenty-First Century*

Introduction: The European Union: Where Next?

With the Millennium fast approaching, there is a wealth of speculation as to the future direction of the Union. Certain areas of Union activity involve a degree of forward planning, moves towards monetary union for example, so predictions here have a basis in fact. Other questions such as a possible accession date of new members into the EU are much less certain. In early 1998, some key indicators are:

- The Franco–German axis remains the driving force within the European Union
- The election of a number of left-wing/socialist governments amongst member states has altered the political complexion of Europe and perhaps enhanced the prospects of European integration
- Refugees continue to seek asylum within member states

Predictions as to what might happen are always risky. This chapter, therefore, rather than trying to make firm predictions, raises some of the questions that will be central to the direction of the European Union, and points out some of the issues that the Union will have to grapple with before the end of the twentieth century in order to move with confidence into the twenty-first.

Even this approach, however, must be recognised for what it is; an attempt to look into as yet unwritten pages of history. Issues have a habit of disappearing the closer you get to them, and hazards that no one has anticipated can prove to be serious stumbling blocks.

None the less, an institution such as the European Union is by its very nature dynamic and cannot stand still, any more than the wider world will cease to develop and change. It is therefore very important to look towards the future, not only in order to be in some measure prepared for whatever it brings, but in order to be able to take a hand in shaping that future.

European Culture

What is 'Culture'?

The promotion of a common European culture is a theme much trumpeted by European Unionists, who hail it as a bond unifying the member states of the Union. This is a difficult contention either to support or to disprove because of the very nature of the word 'culture'. What does it mean? It has to be more than an advanced state of intellectual and aesthetic achievement and must refer to broader points of common interests and values. Paradoxically, it could be argued, the degree of commonality increases the more narrowly one defines culture. Could 15 or 19 or 25 nations profess to share a common culture defined in either of these ways?

Generally, culture is taken to encompass the values and lifestyles that countries enjoy. It includes many elements, among them: tradition, religion and history, heritage, social and sexual mores, ethnicity, attitudes towards children, families and work, acceptance of other races, education, and so on. Not all of these aspects may be common across even a whole member state; attitudes within individual countries can differ radically from one region to another, as seen, for example, in the different responses towards mixed-race marriages in northern and southern France.

Europe does not have a common culture in the sense of identical attitudes held in all member states. However, the member states do share many common bonds and some aspects of culture do cross national borders, weaving into the life of several countries and binding them together.

How Much do Europeans Share?

The question of a common European culture has been used by both sides in the federalism argument, with each side emphasising similarities or differences in order to back up its position.

The federalists point to the 'ties that bind': common factors in the lives of Europeans. The skeptics not only emphasise the differences and make a virtue of diversity, but maintain that this diversity is threatened by the blandness of harmonisation. These arguments are popularised in the UK by a tabloid press anxious to preserve the

British pint and the British sausage from the clutches of Eurocrats who would make us drink beer or milk in 50 centilitre glasses and who would ban the Great British Banger. The Euro-sceptics argue that a British national identity and a European culture are mutually exclusive and that we must choose between them. However, this is not necessarily the case. The example of the USA, where an American culture clearly exists, but where individual states have quite distinct identities and lifestyles (witness the diversity of life between east and west coasts, Florida and New York State), would seem to disprove the sceptics' arguments.

Those who claim that a common European culture exists which unites the Union will find it more difficult to support that claim should the enlargement of the EU become a reality. What cultural factors do the Mediterranean and Eastern European countries have in common with Western Europe? Is a history of democracy a prerequisite to a European culture? It seems unlikely. Culture surely consists of more than political structures. Perhaps we should argue that while these cultures are different, they will be complementary rather than conflicting. The richness and diversity of culture in each of the existing and proposed member states still permits a unity of common cultural threats which cross national boundaries.

Respect for Cultural Differences

Differences between countries do exist and cannot be brushed aside. They can be seen particularly sharply when religion impacts on a country's culture and laws, as, for example, in Ireland's stance on abortion and contraception. The provision in EU law for states to withhold implementation of certain rules, for example, the free movement of people on the grounds of public policy, enables cultural differences to be accommodated. To use the same example, the Irish government does not permit freedom to establish abortion clinics in Ireland on the grounds of public policy, and this exclusion is permitted by the Union.

The mushrooming of satellite TV and pan-European broadcasting is already highlighting the major differences in sexual mores between EU countries. The broadcasting of pornography into countries whose laws forbid such transmissions is an area of dispute. It is likely, however, that member states will always be able to prohibit the broadcast of material considered unacceptable according to their national values.

A Shared Cultural Past – and Future

The ties that bind the European states have existed for over 1000 years. The ecclesiastical culture of the Middle Ages did not respect national boundaries. The art, music, poetry and philosophy which flowered with the great European universities such as Heidelberg, Oxford and Bologna, were fostered by scholars who were at home in any European country.

The links amongst member states are still numerous. There is a common history, a Christian heritage, democratic systems, similar lifestyles and work ethics. It would be argued that the enlargement of the EU may dilute these common factors by admitting countries with non-Christian backgrounds or without a history of liberal democracy. But it could equally be argued that these countries will enrich the EU's culture rather than dilute it.

There is much talk of a youth culture in Europe which transcends national boundaries and which is built on popular music, fashion and the media. Encouraged by the growth of telecommunications, it is a phenomenon which could well spread with the potential enlargement of the EU. It is a potential catalyst for positive growth and for increased unity in the EU. The Union is trying to promote mobility and cultural exchanges among young people in particular, through its funding of exchanges and schemes such as Leonardo and Comenius.

Businesses have long since 'thought European' and identified European customers. The profile of such customers focuses on factors such as age, socio-economic group, income, attitudes, preferences and buying habits; nationality is a minor consideration. Brands such as Benetton and Swatch sit easily on the youth of all member states, as do the computer games they use, the trainers they wear and the soft drinks they consume. The global marketing machines of US and Japanese multinationals have long since targeted a European customer.

There are no easy answers to whether a pan-European culture either exists or is desirable, or whether the enlargement of the EU will encourage or discourage such a phenomenon. What is certain is that European culture has been admired and envied in many parts of the world for centuries and that Europe should be proud of its richness and diversity, promoting this wealth and using it to unify rather than divide.

A Greater Europe

The debate on 'widening versus deepening' within the European Union has moved on. The argument for adding new member states (widening) has been bolstered by the recent accession of Sweden, Austria and Finland. Those who are for the existing member states working together more closely and perhaps moving towards federalism (deepening), are possibly heartened by the likelihood of EMU early in the twenty-first century.

Agenda 2000

This Agenda was published in July 1997 by the European Commission entitled *Agenda 1000: For a stronger and wider Europe*. The document considered all of the existing applications for EU membership in the light of recent events, taking long-term trends into account. It states that 'the priority policy goal of economic and social cohesion must be steadfastly adhered to'. In terms of enlargement, it recommended that negotiations could be started with five states: the Czech Republic, Estonia, Hungary, Poland and Slovenia (Cyprus has already had it confirmed that its application to join will be considered with negotiations to commence late 1997). Ten countries currently wish to join the EU.

Apart from economic convergence, the EU also requires significant improvement from potential new members in five key areas: anti-crime measures, agriculture, transport, energy policies and the environment. Requirements are:

- Public administration, justice and domestic policies must all adhere to EU standards
- All nuclear reactors must meet EU safety standards
- Measures to be adopted to ensure the safety of people and property and to fight crime
- Governments to be vigilant in their campaigns against organised crime, corruption, terrorism and illegal immigration

Europe and the Environment

Four key European Union states, France, Germany, Italy and the UK, were unable to persuade the USA, Japan and Canada to take tougher measures at home to cut carbon emissions. Despite its poor reputation on environmental issues (the USA accounts for 25 per cent of world greenhouse gases), the USA was able to deflect demands made by the four European countries made at the G7 Summit held in 1997. A compromise was agreed which fell short of both European standards and hopes.

The EU had agreed a target of 15 per cent reduction for carbon emission cuts by 2010, but the G7 countries were unable to agree to these targets. The Europeans were not happy with the results. Chancellor Helmut Kohl commented, 'The Europeans are simply further along'.

European Commission President, Jacques Santer, said, 'I am

frankly disappointed that not all our partners were able here and now to take quantified commitments on the reduction of greenhouse-gas emissions. We must stop the degradation of our climate. The future of the planet is at stake.'

The French President, Jacques Chirac, whose own country has a good record on greenhouse-gas emissions, pulled no punches at the end of the Summit. Referring to the Americans, he declared, 'They pollute enormously'.

The communiqué issued at the end of the Summit spoke of 'meaningful, realistic and equitable targets' without stating a figure. The challenge to the USA and others was laid down clearly by Tony Blair. 'We in Europe have put our cards on the table,' he declared, referring to Washington. 'It's time for the special pleading to stop and for others to follow suit.'

Whilst environmental issues remain important for the European Union, the member states are clearly impacted by their global partners. It is likely that the four European G7 members will continue to pressure their partners at future summits.

EMU . . . What Next?

Those countries wishing to join the single currency will be examined by the EMI in the spring of 1998 to determine whether they meet the convergence criteria. The latest available European Commission forecast of October 1997, predicted that only Greece would fail to meet the criteria. Only Denmark, Sweden and Britain are likely to rule out joining in the first wave which commences in 1999, leading up to the abolition of the currencies of participating countries in 2002. The ability of countries wishing to join to maintain their economies satisfactorily during 1998 will be a requirement.

The UK's position has been altered by the new Labour government elected in May 1997. Entry has been ruled out before the next general election (2002) and it has been indicated that a referendum will be held to determine whether Britain enters.

Index